HELP!

for the SMALL MUSEUM

A Handbook of Exhibit Ideas and Methods

by

Arminta Neal, Curator

Department of Graphic Design
Denver Museum of Natural History

Pruett Publishing ● Boulder, Colorado

8   9   10

Library of Congress Catalog Card Number 70-75438

ISBN: 0-87108-138-5

PRINTED IN THE UNITED STATES OF AMERICA

DEDICATED to the memory of

FREDERIC H. (Eric) DOUGLAS

former Director and Curator
of American Indian Art and
Native Arts of the Denver
Art Museum.

FOREWORD

Everywhere in this country people in small museums seem to be hungry for specific and helpful information about how to assemble and care for the collections which they need, and even hungrier for information about how to exhibit these collections most effectively. Yet, in the face of this often-expressed need, relatively little has been put into print on the subject. There have been occasional papers presented at national and regional meetings, occasional seminars and workshops which reached a few people in a few areas, and occasional articles, usually in journals of modest circulation. Now, after two decades of experience, Arminta Neal has addressed herself to this book about the problem.

She is a remarkable person. I have heard someone else say of her (and justly) that she is the only museum designer he knows who takes a visitor proudly into a new gallery and says, "See how little we spent here," instead of, "See how much we spent here." She is a better-than-ordinary folk singer, an ingenious technician, a photographic expert both with the camera and in the darkroom, an enthusiastic and effective lecturer, an inventive exhibits designer who knows how to keep the design from overwhelming material exhibited—and a warm and attractive personality with friends all over the country. In addition to her full-time job as exhibits designer for one of the great natural history museums in this country, she has taken on (often out of pure enthusiasm and at real disadvantage to herself) a multitude of formal and informal consultations with smaller museums and even individual exhibitions. No one I know, East or West, is so effective in pointing out that good exhibition is not so much a matter of money as a matter of ingenuity and in isolating and explaining the principles which are basic to the matter.

This book is the outgrowth of a developmental series of professional papers and articles and represents the jelling of ideas that comes with long familiarity. Its pages contain concepts that have been talked over and tried out and taught in a variety of situations; ideas that have turned out to be effective and practical in actual use; and, most important of all, ideas that are within the reach of a small organization, even one without any paid staff. These ideas are, I think, going to meet a widespread need among American museums—and not only among the smaller ones.

H. J. Swinney, Director

Adirondack Museum
Blue Mountain Lake, N.Y.
1968

CONTENTS

INTRODUCTION and ACKNOWLEDGMENTS

In October of 1955 a slide lecture, "Gallery and Case Exhibit Design," was prepared by the author for the Ohio State Historical Society. The lecture later was published in mimeographed form and was soon out of print. Reprinting by the Ohio Society and the Clearinghouse Newsletter for Western Museums was followed by revision and publication in *Curator*. Throughout the years, additional articles were presented at various workshops and conferences and in professional journals. In 1966, all articles were collected into one mimeographed booklet, "Help! for Small Museums." This collection has been out of print for more than a year. The present book represents an extensive re-writing and expansion effort.

While the original articles were developed specifically with the small museum in mind (those with low budgets and staffed essentially by volunteers), the principles apply equally to larger institutions.

The writer is grateful to *Curator* (published by the American Museum of Natural History) for permission to reprint material presented in the articles "Gallery and Case Exhibit Design" and "Function of Display: Regional Museums" which appeared in that quarterly in Vol. VI, No. 1, 1963, and Vol. VIII, No. 3, 1965. She also wishes to express thanks to *History News* (monthly newsletter of the American Association for State and Local History) for permission to include material published as their Technical Leaflets Nos. 22 and 23.

Many people have provided assistance and encouragement in the preparation of the original articles and the resulting publications and the writer wishes to thank: William T. Alderson, Robert L. Akerley, Stephan F. de Borhegyi, George Bowditch, Willena D. Cartwright, Edwin H. Colbert, Frederick J. Dockstader, James Grady, J. Keever Greer, Carl Guthe, Richard S. Hagen, Louise C. Harrison, Eugene Kingman, G. Carroll Lindsay, Alice Marriott, William Marshall, Hugo Rodeck, Clement Silvestro, H. J. Swinney, Harry Shapiro, Stanley Sohl, and Marvin Tong.

Special thanks for editorial assistance go to Doris E. Samford.

Part I:

GENERAL PRINCIPLES

FUNCTION OF DISPLAY

A recent magazine article discusses statistics of interest to the museum profession which were compiled originally by the Bureau of Outdoor Recreation Survey and the Outdoor Recreation Resources Review Commission.[1]

The paper reveals that the number of sightseers in the country in 1965 (some 457 million people) is expected to increase by the year 2000 to 1 billion, 169 million -- a gain of 156%.

The museum world is also growing by leaps and bounds. Currently there are some 5,000 museums in the United States -- over a thousand more than there were in 1950. New museums open at the astounding rate of one every three and a half days.[2]

Today with travel and television, people are generally better informed about their world and have broader interests than previous generations. They are interested in the "whys" and "hows" of things certainly as much as they are in the "whats" -- and by the "whats" I mean the objects in museum collections.

In older days when communications were slow -- when it took a long time to go from "here" to "there" -- most folks didn't travel and the curiosities of the world, the *objects* of collections, commanded great interest. Scientific knowledge about the world was increasing rapidly and expeditions were sent out to explore, collect and return home with as many rare, new and unclassified specimens as was possible. Sorting out and investigation of the specimens could follow later. The important thing was to collect.

The collecting "instinct" (it might be termed) is an old one. At least 40,000 years ago and perhaps as much as 85,000 years ago, man was a collector for archaeologists, investigating in the caves of Neanderthal men, have found pieces of red ochre, fossil shells and peculiarly-shaped stones.[3] These collections of curiosities possibly represent the oldest known "curio cabinets" as museums in their earliest history have been called.

Early museums were often the private collections of princes, nobles, and wealthy patrons of the arts and sciences and reflected the specialized interests of these people. Seldom open to the public, they were prestige items which one showed off to friends (being sure that all objects collected were placed on view). Having an extensive gallery or curio cabinet confirmed that the owner had the wealth, position and power either to acquire the objects on personal tours of strange places, or was able to send emissaries on exploring and collecting expeditions. The results of these tours -- *all* materials collected -- often found their way into the equivalent of a huge trophy room.

Greatest Butterfly Collection in America

"Ornamental Entomology", 1909

Many museums today, large and small, have not progressed beyond this stage of museum exhibit evolution and are frozen in the suspended animation of display techniques that developed in the late 1700's.

Recently I travelled from Denver to the West Coast, to the Mid-West and to the East Coast and in each area it was often possible to anticipate the exhibits of small museums before entering the buildings. I could be sure there would be department-store display cases with glass tops, fronts and sides, and with sliding glass doors at the back. The cases would be lined with glass shelves which would create a series of monotonously repetitive lines in the main room. The quantity of glass surfaces would reflect light from every available source in the room. In one case there would be a collection of china with, in some instances, dinner plates stacked one on top

5

of another.   In another there would be neatly folded linens.

In yet another there might be twenty to fifty moustache cups.
Somewhere there would be a table type of case with a scratched

glass top and inside would be hundreds of chipped stone points,
scrapers, choppers, knives, and hammerstones.   Another table

case would have some bedraggled stuffed birds (probably from Asia or Africa). Additional cases would be
filled with clothing, carpenter's tools, blacksmithing
equipment, dentist's picks, a doctor's bag, and old
office equipment. Guns would be stacked from floor
to ceiling and bullets, cartridge cases, bullet molds and
cans of gunpowder would be on one of the glass shelves in
any of the previously mentioned cases. All items would
be identified with a typewritten caption on a white index
card.

These museums from coast to coast, are exhibiting
their materials in what has come to be called the "visible
storage" type of display, much like the cans on the
shelves of a supermarket. Their efforts often resemble
those of department stores, with the glass-topped, glass-
sided cases edged with gleaming metal trim resting on
rich hardwood bases aligned in even rows that march
across the expanse of the display room. Reflections on
the myriad surfaces of glass prevent immediate recognition of the contents of the cases, so that the room becomes

a place where the glass display cases themselves are the immediate objects shown, not the items inside them. Sometimes, the only apparent difference is that in one instance items are accompanied by a price tag and in the other they are accompanied by a donor tag, e.g., "This lace handkerchief carried across the Plains in 1869 by Eliza Brown, donated in loving memory by her granddaughter, Mrs. Edward Smith."

The first function of a museum today is still to collect, document, and preserve those materials within its stated province -- be it natural history, history, art, science, or industry. We want to collect the objects representing our history, not only to preserve the nostalgia of time past for older citizens, but to inspire young people with a feeling for history. We want to be able to interest our youngsters in our heritage, but, because they *are* youngsters, they will not understand the objects of history if these are not interpreted. And so we come to the second basic function of a museum which is *to select items* from its collections and, in displaying them, *organize them into a meaningful story.*

For the small museum this function carries with it the responsibility of exhibiting the *local* story *first* and in depth. This is why people have come to the museum -- to learn about the area in which it is located, not to see another collection-on-view which may differ only slightly from a collection they have seen the day before in a different locale. All the components of a collection -- the relics, the mineral specimens, business journals, old guns, natural history specimens -- all these things of the local area will, of themselves, tell the visitor nothing. They *do* provide the raw material on which interpretation is based. They also provide a visual impact on the mind of the viewer,

creating concrete and tangible images that are remembered
longer than a skillful illustration in a book. But to
communicate, this raw material must be adequately labeled
and arranged to present a logical sequence. Some of the
questions in the visitors' minds which exhibits might
answer would be:

WHERE is the town or region; what is its relationship to the surrounding areas?

WHY is the town where it is? In the west this
question might be answered in a number of ways: "We're
where cattle trails crossed; where the railroad ended
for ten years before moving on; where Indians camped
and trappers came to trade; where a stage station was
located on the old Santa Fe or Oregon trails; where
prospectors came to search for gold and silver and
merchants followed to establish businesses." In the
east this question might be answered by one of the
following: "We're where a fort was built during the
French and Indian War; on a river that was the first
'highway' through the country and a portage was necessary at this point; the coastline made the start of a
safe harbor and fishing was good; trade ships from
Europe transferred goods here for inland distribution."
It might even be answered with "We're where recreational use of the area developed early and people came to
enjoy hiking, fishing, hunting, and camping."

Additional questions to be answered by exhibits are:

WHO came here first? What Indians were here? How
did they live? What did they eat and how did they get
it? How was the food prepared, with what kind of
utensils? What kind of houses did they build? What
style of clothing did they wear? Who were their

9

enemies before Europeans appeared on the scene?

WHO were the first EUROPEANS in the area: explorers, soldiers, traders?

WHO were the first SETTLERS? Where did they come from? Why? How many came? Where did they *first* settle? How many stayed?

Not only should the questions of "where", "why" (originally) and "who" be answered by the small museum's exhibits, but also "Why does the town *still* exist?" Is it one that depends upon lumbering or its affiliated industries, pulp, paper, plyboard or chipboard? Is it on the coast with a good harbor and a thriving shipbuilding industry that has changed from making schooners to submarines? Is it a major shipping point for cattle? Is it in the midst of a major recreational area? Museum visitors will be interested in the businesses and industries of the region -- their history and development and present-day methods of operation.

Almost always there will be one or more incidents which are unique to the local area represented by the small museum and while they may not have had much bearing on the main course of national history, they are interesting simply as illustrations of the problems people have faced in former times. Use of the objects in collections to help explain these incidents will aid the visitor in remembering a specific museum over others which simply place the materials with others of their kind on the glass shelves in their display cases.

There is, of course, a place for the quantities of so-called duplicate items in any collection. This place is the study collection, which is rarely placed on public exhibition, but is made available to students and scholars who may need many examples of a given object for comparison in their investigations. Study collections are often arranged much like the stacks in a library and work tables with appropriate lights are provided at regular intervals for the use of research visitors. These research visitors are the ones who will appreciate and use the great masses of materials that are not placed on public display.

The ultimate aim of any museum exhibit, whether in a large or small institution, should be to stimulate such an interest in the subject that the viewer wishes to learn more about it in his spare time.

[1] "The Big Leisure-Time Explosion," in Popular Gardening and Living Outdoors, Spring, 1968, Holt, Rinehart and Winston, Inc.

[2] Schwartz, Alvin, Museum: The Story of America's Treasure Houses, E.P. Dutton & Co., Inc., 1967, pg. 18.

[3] Leroi-Gourhan, A., Prehistoric Man, Philosophical Library, New York, 1957, pg. 41.

EVOLUTION OF A GALLERY

In May, 1909, a series of mineral exhibits, housed in the then Colorado Museum of Natural History, was opened to the public.

Denver Municipal Facts, May 22, 1909

An Interior Showing Arrangement of Curio Cabinets in Museum at City Park.

Denver Municipal Facts, Nov. 13, 1909

By November, 1909, additional floor cases had been purchased and installed. The two mineral "pyramids" in the previous picture are barely visible in the back portion of the room.

In the early 1950's the vertical portions of the floor cases had been removed but the floor was still pretty well covered by the "visible storage" kind of exhibit. By this time the name of the institution had changed to the Denver Museum of Natural History.

In the late 1950's the floor
cases were removed and a process of selection of materials
was under way. Extra specimens were retired to a study
collection.

By the early 1960's alcoves with
built-in cases were designed to
enclose many of the pillars in
the room and materials were installed to tell the chronological
story of the "Succession of Life."

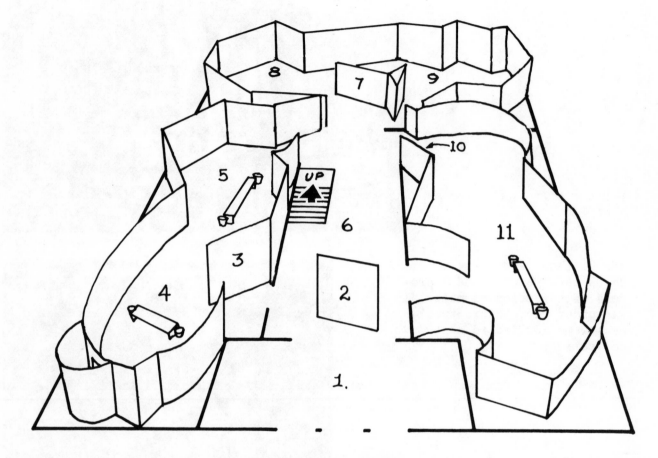

FIRST FLOOR PLAN for Functional Outline of a Museum

FUNCTIONAL OUTLINE OF A TYPICAL WESTERN MUSEUM

The following outline illustrates the layout
of a medium-sized imaginary museum of history in a
non-existent western state which might be organized
along the functional interpretive lines just discussed. These concepts of interpretation may be used
whether the displays are arranged in alcoves, because
of restricted space, or in a series of separate rooms.
(Numbers on the drawing correlate with numbers in the
outline.)

The visitor, entering our imaginary museum,
would find himself in what can be called a reception
area (1), with an information desk and an attendant at
one side. This reception section could include a small
book and gift shop where items appropriate to the exhibits in the museum would be on sale. Across the room
could be a checking stand where coats, packages, bundles,
brief cases, and other hindrances to the physical comfort
of the visitor could be safely stored, without charge,
for the duration of the visit. Other facilities immediately apparent, and perhaps adjacent to the checking stand,
would be a pay telephone, a drinking fountain, and rest
rooms. Several benches or comfortable chairs, with con-
venient ash trays, placed around the area, could provide
a meeting place and also permit smoking in an area under
constant supervision by the information attendant.

Directly opposite the entrance, just within a
hall leading to the rest of the museum, a large panel (2)
reaching, perhaps from floor to ceiling, could carry a
label that might read as follows:

IN OUR MUSEUM YOU MAY SEE THE STORY OF OUR LOCAL
HISTORY. On this floor there are three main display rooms:

The Natural History Background and the
Earliest In habitants -- the Indians
(to the left of the main corridor)

Early Explorers and Travelers (in the
room straight ahead at the end of
the corridor)

Permanent Settlements: Development of towns
with industries, agriculture, transportation
and communication (to the right of the main
corridor)

Second floor exhibits show the development of our
community since the transition from Territory to
present-day State.

The Museum also owns extensive study collections of
historical objects, photographs and manuscripts which
are available to scholars and students upon application.

WE HOPE YOU ENJOY YOUR VISIT

Now the visitor may make a choice. If he is
interested primarily in how the early farmers of the
area lived, he can go directly to the third gallery
and digest its contents before "museum fatigue" sets in.
Let us suppose, however, that he wishes to see the whole
story. He proceeds to the first gallery -- the one to
the left of the main corridor.

Just inside its entrance may be another large panel (3)
with oversize photographs of landscapes typical of the area.
The label might read:

A VARIETY OF LANDFORMS AND ACCOMPANYING CLIMATES
has made it possible for a great number of plants
and animals to live in our State since before remembered time. In the earliest days of human
occupation, Indians followed the herds of game, and
animals and men lived together without competition.

By its position, this panel would direct the visitor

into the room (4) where he might find selected exhibits summarizing the main species of plants and animals found in the area (of particular interest if the visitor is camping on his trip), and additional exhibits tracing the development of Indian cultures up to the time of contact with the white man (5). Several visual techniques could be distributed through the room: relief maps, photographs of specimens of plants and animals, together with miniature dioramas depicting ecological associations; artifacts, and explanatory panels. The exhibits would stress natural history as the background for the local history showing, for example, how animal trails were followed by later explorers.

Chairs or benches would be so placed as to permit resting while viewing, and at the end of each bench there would be a large waste basket in which film cartons, Polaroid camera clutter, and other litter could be deposited. Returning to the central corridor (6), the visitor would proceed to the second gallery.

Again, an introductory panel (7) would display a very large map of the area with the trails followed by early explorers marked in relation to present-day towns and highways. The label on this panel might read:

SPANISH EXPLORERS CROSSED OUR LAND AS EARLY AS 1604 searching for gold and for new routes to the Pacific Coast. In 1830 the first fur trappers, the famous "Mountain Men", were the first Americans to explore land which, at that time, did not yet belong to the United States.

Exhibits in this section (8) would include detailed maps of the routes of explorers and trappers, displays of such artifacts as would show how the early Spanish soldiers were equipped for such rough service; artifacts that would,

with proper labeling, illustrate the life of the early
trappers and explain their methods of trapping, supply
and freighting; and cases containing trade goods with
labels explaining the value of each in trade -- e.g.,
how many beaver pelts could be secured in exchange for
a metal tomahawk.

Additional exhibits (9) would explain the routes
and hardships endured by the early American military ex-
plorations -- groups such as those led by John C. Fremont
and Zebulon Pike. Other exhibits would show what emigrant
trails, if any, crossed the area.

Finally, on this first floor, the visitor would
enter the third gallery. Here the introductory panel (10)
might have an opening cut into it which might frame a
diorama representing a wagon train. The main label would
explain:

> PERMANENT SETTLEMENT OF OUR AREA BEGAN WHEN EMIGRANTS
> FROM THE EAST, lured by the prospect of rich farming
> lands, banded together in wagon trains to make the
> hazardous trek across the Plains and Mountains.

Exhibits in the gallery (11) might follow an outline
such as the following:

THE FIRST ARRIVALS: 1850 - 1860

> Displays might include tools and equipment used
> during a wagon train trip. Labels might be drawn
> from various pioneer diaries. A "Who's Who" of
> daguerreotypes showing some of the early settlers
> could be included.

EARLY COMMUNITIES

> How the People Lived and Worked: Man's Work, Woman's
>   Work (could be arranged according to the calendar)

> Home Life: Social Life: Home entertainment, Balls
>   Parties, Celebrations (such as Fourth of July)

Schools

Churches

Early Stores and Industries

Indian Troubles

Military Forts and the Soldier's Life

COMMUNICATION WITH THE "OUTSIDE WORLD"

Freight and mail routes; timetables and rates

Pony express days

Completion of the Transcontinental Telegraph

THE COMING OF THE RAILROAD: A new day of rapid
development and the end of Pioneer times

Second floor displays could depict the partici-
pation of the community in the Civil War, the Spanish-
American War, First and Second World Wars, and in the
Korean and Vietnam Wars; it would also detail the lives
of local residents who were important in national affairs.
A centrally located room with adjacent rest rooms, and a
drinking fountain, would again give the visitor an opportunity to relax before continuing his viewing of the
exhibits.

In all the galleries outlined a variety of techniques would be used to provide a visual change of pace
for the visitor to help counteract the inevitable fatigue.
These techniques, some of which have already been mentioned,
would include:

Panels

Maps

Case openings of various sizes and shapes

19

Automatic slide projectors with rear-projection
screens or animated scrolls; either device to
be provided with two or three rows of benches
to permit sitting while viewing

Variations in ceiling height and floor levels where
possible within structure of the building

Change of pace in presentation of very large (Conestoga wagon) and very small objects (snuff boxes)

If the labels accompanying these exhibits are
written to convey something of the strengths and weaknesses,
sorrows and delights of the people who used the objects
displayed and also impart the statistical information relating to dates and places, and, if these labels have been
kept short and to the point, the visitor will retain some
of the idea of sequence and flow of the history of the
region and may even be stimulated to pursue some facet of
the story in greater depth. If this happens, the *full*
function of the museum's displays has been achieved. For,
though educational, the exhibits cannot, from a practical
standpoint of observer time involved, explore any one
subject in depth. The exhibits should so excite the visitor
that he leaves determined to learn in some way more about
the detail that has intrigued him.

PLANNING MUSEUM DISPLAYS

Museum exhibits, whether a single case or an entire hall, essentially are a means of communication. In order to communicate successfully the person planning the exhibit should be thoroughly familiar with five factors. These are:

1. the idea or story to be told;

2. the objects with which to tell it;

3. the area or space to be devoted to the story (size, dimension, shape);

4. an awareness of the audience it is to reach;

5. and a knowledge of available cases and panels, of building materials and design techniques with which to present the story.

THE STORY

The importance of the story to be told has already been emphasized in previous chapters. Planning the manner in which the information is to be conveyed (whether a single case or a total gallery is involved) must not be a hit-or-miss effort or just the "lumping" together of similar objects within an area. People who read Reader's Digest or a collection of short stories may remember one or two articles or stories vividly but completely forget the remainder. The same people who read a novel -- even one that is badly written -- will remember the setting, the main characters, their inter-relationships, and the plot, for all are tied together in a unit. So must the exhibit be a unit, and the individual parts must contribute to that unit if communication from the specialist to the visitor, via the exhibit, is to be achieved.

The first step toward accomplishing this unification is perhaps the most difficult to take: write a specific and precise outline of the main points that are to be covered.

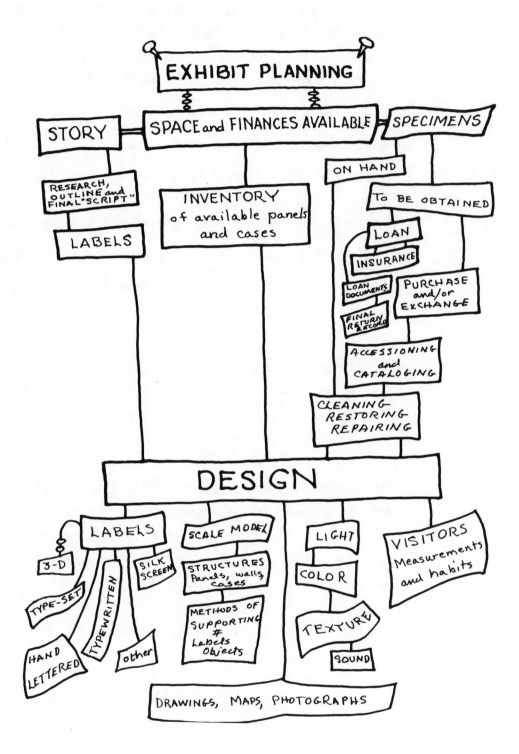

EXHIBIT PLANNING

STORY   SPACE and FINANCES AVAILABLE   SPECIMENS

RESEARCH, OUTLINE and FINAL "SCRIPT"

LABELS

INVENTORY of available panels and cases

ON HAND

TO BE OBTAINED

LOAN

INSURANCE

LOAN DOCUMENTS

FINAL RETURN RECORD

PURCHASE and/or EXCHANGE

ACCESSIONING and CATALOGING

CLEANING RESTORING REPAIRING

DESIGN

LABELS

3-D

TYPE-SET

HAND LETTERED

TYPEWRITTEN

other

SILK SCREEN

SCALE MODEL

STRUCTURES Panels, walls, cases

METHODS OF SUPPORTING # Labels Objects

LIGHT

COLOR

TEXTURE

SOUND

VISITORS Measurements and habits

DRAWINGS, MAPS, PHOTOGRAPHS

It is easy for one to speak in general terms and wave one's hands in the air saying, "We'll put the Indian stuff here at the entrance to the hall and about mid-way we'll put what's left of that old Conestoga wagon to introduce the Pioneer Section."

But to commit a logical sequence to paper is most difficult. As topics are written down, additional subjects demand attention, and the rearranging of these basic considerations becomes a disagreeable chore. One approach is to list individual elements on index cards with a headline phrase. Secondary facts relating to the main elements also may be jotted down on the cards. After all conceivable elements have been listed, the cards may be arranged and re-arranged until a satisfactory sequence is obtained. When the set of cards is compared with the amount of space available for the exhibit, it may be determined if some elements must be discarded or expanded. The information on the cards becomes a workable "script" from which design may proceed and preliminary labels may be written. A final planning script should indicate (as does a script prepared for television) those "visuals" -- specimens, artifacts, models, dioramas, maps, photographs, drawings, paintings -- which will be required to illustrate the concepts set forth. This script will make it possible to determine what structures (panels or cases) are required for each section.

The following two sample scripts illustrate how an outline may be prepared.

SAMPLE EXHIBIT SCRIPT (1)

OUTLINE

RED MEN HALL MUSEUM, Empire, Colorado
(Empire Conservation Society)

Note: Most PANELS with DIORAMAS eventually to be modified to CASES
with dioramas and historical specimens

	Kind of exhibit	Materials to use	Contents of labels
1.	PANEL at entrance	Relief map	The Setting: Rocky Mountain Continental Divide; minerals; present-day proximity to fishing and skiing areas
2.	PANEL with diorama	Diorama and mural-size photo	Cowles and Graves sight possible way through Continental Divide barrier (later to be Berthoud Pass)
3.	PANEL with diorama	Diorama	"EUREKA" -- discovery of surface gold by Cowles and Freeman
4.	CASE	Single figure miniature showing use of rocker, gold pan, pick, quicksilver flask, balance, nugget	Early mining methods: Recovery of surface gold
5.	PANEL with diorama	Diorama	North Empire in 1863 (from Library of Congress photo)
6.	PANEL	Photo blow-ups (taken from old map decorative border)	Later mining methods: (forced by dwindling of surface materials)
7.	CASE with diorama set in back panel	Diorama showing shaft and tunnel development, use of burros; burro pack saddle and shoes, miner's candle holder	Shaft and tunnel mining and importance of burro to early operations
8.	CASE	Rock and mineral specimens	Rocks and Minerals of the Empire District
9.	PANEL with diorama	Diorama	Minnesota Mines about 1940; last and greatest of the gold mining operations at Empire

Kind of exhibit	Materials to use	Contents of labels
10. CASE with diorama set in back panel	Diorama and old ice skates	Winter sports in the early town
11. PANEL with diorama	Diorama	Summer activities: berry picking
12. PANEL with diorama	Diorama	Summer activities: going to Ice Tunnel for ice
13. PANEL with diorama	Diorama	Summer activities: beer keg-lifting contest
14. PANEL with diorama	Diorama	Ute Indians camped in Empire valley awaiting distribution of annuities
15. PANEL with diorama	Diorama (Town Hall Ball)	Use of Town Hall for various recreational pursuits
16. PANEL with diorama	Diorama	First race track in Clear Creek County
17. PANEL with diorama	Diorama (Toll Gate House)	Building of wagon road over Berthoud Pass
18. PANEL (rear of introductory panel)	Photos and photo-copy of early newspaper	One hundred years of travel over Berthoud Pass; avalanche hazards
19. PANEL	Prints and photos	Early and present-day ski scenes

FLOOR EXHIBITS:

On central post: Miners' carbide lamps

Platform around central post: Location for bulky objects (changed from time to time): wooden ore car; metal ore bucket; home-made wheelbarrow (shown in miniature in Ice Tunnel diorama)

SAMPLE EXHIBIT SCRIPT (2)

CASE EXHIBIT in PALEONTOLOGY SERIES, Denver Museum of Natural History

Location in case	Material to use	Contents of labels
Back panel	(Headline label; 3-D letters)	About 300 million years ago, in THE PENNSYLVANIAN PERIOD, coal was deposited on the greatest scale in the earth's history.
Back panel	(Sub-head; 3-D letters)	A profusion of vegetation flourished in vast fresh water swamps, resulting in the famous coal deposits of Pennsylvania, from which the geologic period has been named.
Back panel	Large painting of Coal Age swamp with large amphibian (Diplovertebron) in foreground	Marine invertebrates were prolific and varied. In the swamps many kinds of amphibians slithered and sprawled from pool to pool, preying upon other amphibians, spiders, centipedes, scorpions, cockroaches, and a variety of winged insects.
Back panel	Map of mid-Penn. Period	RECURRING PATTERNS OF SEDIMENTATION recorded in Pennsylvanian deposits are an outstanding geologic feature of the period.
Right side of case, on panel	(Topic sentence of PLANT GROUP labels)	PLANTS of the COAL FORESTS generally were similar to those of late Devonian and Mississippian times but were more luxuriant and abundant.
Mounted on case furniture on floor of case	Specimens available: Catalogue No. 907: stigmaria, No. 928, 931, 920: to be removed from Mazon Creek case and re-installed: Nos. 1518, 1511, 1517, 1519	The SCALE TREES were the most imposing plants of the humid forests. They had straight, high trunks, unbranched except near the top, and grew to heights of one hundred feet. When the leaves were shed, they left permanent scars which gave the bark a scaly appearance and this is the characteristic for which the trees have been named. They reproduced by means of spores. Most belonged to one of two well-defined groups: Lepidodendron or Sigillaria. Today, scale trees and club mosses are represented by a few groups descended from their more numerous Paleozoic ancestors.

In preparing the exhibit script the planner must remember the museum visitor has physical limitations. Multi-media notwithstanding, if a visitor's feet ache or if his back hurts, he will leave an exhibit in the middle of the room, and confusion created by a mass assault on his senses will send him forth without comprehending the exhibit's content. Display also has its limitations. It can impress a viewer and help him to remember general conclusions; rarely can it convey complicated and extensive information. These facts should be left to printed leaflets or guides.

THE OBJECTS

While the story is being worked out in an exhibit script, the materials with which it will be interpreted are gathered together. Continuing to recognize the limitations of display, the planner must resist the temptation to put a study or storage collection on view, for some observers have noted that most people spend no more than from thirty to forty-five seconds viewing a single display. In this brief time, the visitor is expected to see all objects and retain all information about them. He cannot do this if he is overwhelmed with material and deluged with labels. Materials must be selected for the purpose of best illustrating the idea being presented. A list of actual specimens on hand should be made and objects requiring it should be cleaned, repaired and restored to make them ready for exhibition. A list should be made of those things which must be obtained elsewhere by purchase, exchange or loan. If there is a gap of visual materials, it should be decided if drawings, photographs, or reconstructions will serve, and the preparation of these items should be scheduled.

No. 1 X-Acto Knife with No. 11 blade

SOME of the TOOLS USED

IN MAKING SCALE MODELS

T - Square

30°/60°   45°/90°

Plastic triangles

Dressmaker's pins with colored
rounded heads (easier on fingers
than standard head)

Architect's triangular scale ruler

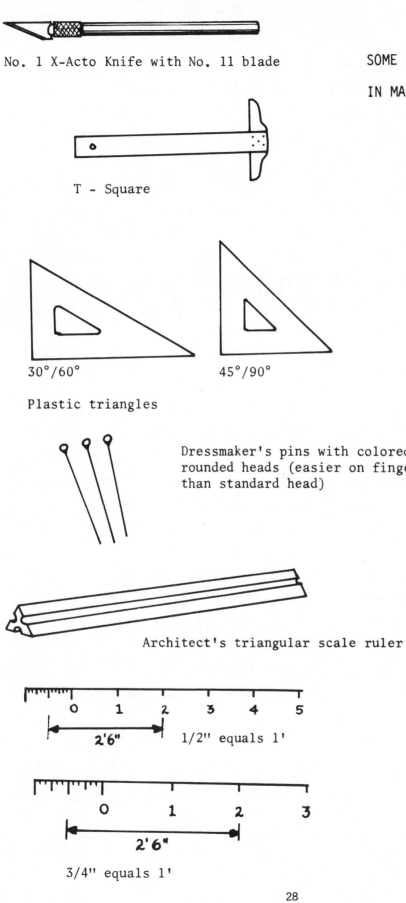

2'6"   1/2" equals 1'

2'6"

3/4" equals 1'

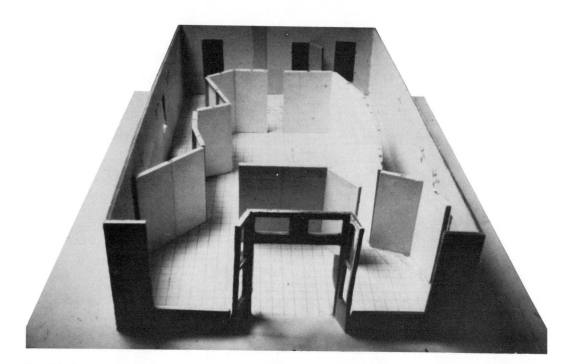

Preliminary model   RED MEN HALL MUSEUM,   Empire, Colorado
Scale: 1/2" = 1'   Panels of file-folder cardboard re-
                           inforced with balsa wood frames.

THE SPACE AVAILABLE: Making and Using a Scale Model

Both the extent of the story and the amount of
material used will be governed by the space made available
for the exhibit. At this point in planning the use of a
scale model is a great time-saver. The model need not be
elaborate.

Use a piece of 1/4" plyboard or Upson board for a
base. For scale panels use light weight cardboard such
as that in file folders or index cards reinforcing where
needed with balsa wood strips glued to the cardboard with
Elmer's glue. Use straight pins to hold pieces together
until the glue dries.

A list of tools for making scale models would include: A No. 1 X-Acto knife with a No. 11 blade, a small
T-square, plastic triangles, a metal-edged ruler (to be
used as a guide when cutting the cardboard), and an architect's triangular scale ruler. Be sure the triangular ruler
is one divided for architects (in fractions) and not one

29

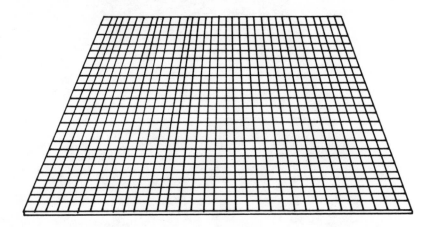

Lay out floor plan graph on base

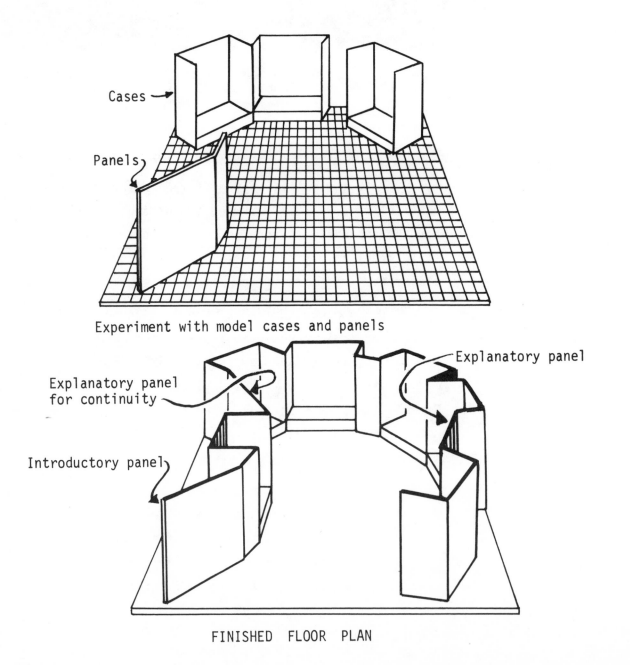

Cases

Panels

Experiment with model cases and panels

Explanatory panel

Explanatory panel
for continuity

Introductory panel

FINISHED FLOOR PLAN

divided for engineers (in units of 10, 20, 30, etc.).
It should be possible to purchase all of these tools
from an art supply store or the art department of an
office supply store.

To make a scale model of a gallery, use either
the 1/2" to 1' or the 3/4" to 1' scale and draw a graph
of squares on the base piece, then draw in the floor
plan of the room which is to be used. Be sure to indicate the presence of windows and doors and the direction in which doors open. It is also a good idea to
draw in the location of electric outlets.

Use the light-weight cardboard and
balsa wood to make individual models of the
proposed panels and cases, floor platforms,
and any other exhibit structures which will
be used. These individual models need not
be detailed -- just something to give the
correct idea of bulk and floor
space requirements. Cut out
a scale figure (the 1/2" to
1' and 3/4" to 1' are shown
here) using lightweight
cardboard; glue a small
scrap of cardboard to the
base so the figure will
stand. Use of this figure
will help to visualize the
cases and panels in relation
to the visitor's size.

1/2" scale   3/4" scale

By moving these model cases and panels around the
plyboard base and correlating their placement with the
written outline, the floor plan will develop. Using a scale

model aids in designing a traffic pattern which will be easy for visitors to follow and gives the specialist (historian or scientist) a concrete idea as to how the display will be handled. Use of a model permits both the specialist and designer to correct any aspect of the presentation that seems wrong and gives everyone concerned a realistic approach to determining costs, for on the scale model it can be seen where existing cases and panels may be used and where new structures must be made.

Models of individual cases are helpful when designing single exhibits. Pebble-board (available from art stores) is a good weight of cardboard to use, and a scale of 1 1/2" to 1' gives a model large enough to be able to determine location and area occupied by both labels and specimens, and permits making miniature replicas of the case "furniture" -- the boxes, pedestals, shelves -- that will be required. By working with the model the specialist and designer may come to a compromise in deciding if some story material must be edited further and some specimens discarded, or if an additional case must be added to the total plan to provide needed space.

THE MUSEUM "AUDIENCE"

The museum audience is neither specialized nor captive but consists of such extremes as school children and scholars, Sunday strollers and tourists. Even if the designer considers every behaviour rule he has ever learned, some atypical visitors will confound traffic patterns, ignoring in their own observation of the displays every attempt by the designer to direct and guide their attention.

The designer's basic planning should include a recognition of some physical facts about people. If visitors have headaches, bloodshot eyes, tired backs, sagging arches and burning feet after they have seen the Museum's exhibits, the designer has forgotton to consider how people are built.

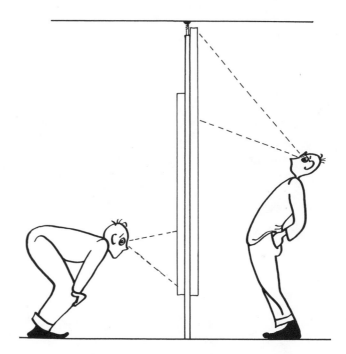

The man on the left is having trouble because detailed things more than three feet below his eye level are difficult to see. The man on the right is having equal difficulty with a label that is more than one foot above his eye level. If either man is wearing bifocals he probably will abandon any effort to see the exhibit rather than acquire an uncomfortable crick in his neck.

With little eye movement, people usually see and recognize with ease things that are within an approximately

elliptical cone of vision
(illustrated here) with
the apex of the cone at
eye-level height. Limits
of *comfortable* head movements are shown below.

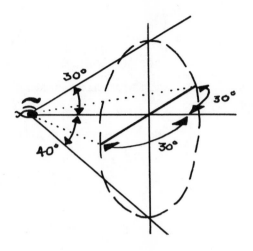

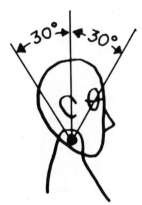

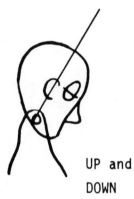

COMFORTABLE head movements

UP and
DOWN

from SIDE to SIDE

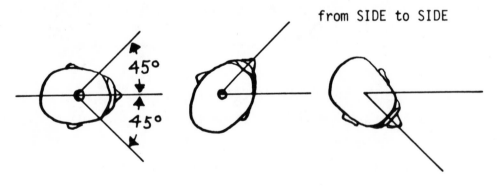

Arranging objects and labels beyond these visual
and physical limitations will place a strain on seldom-
used muscles and produce a severe case of museum fatigue.

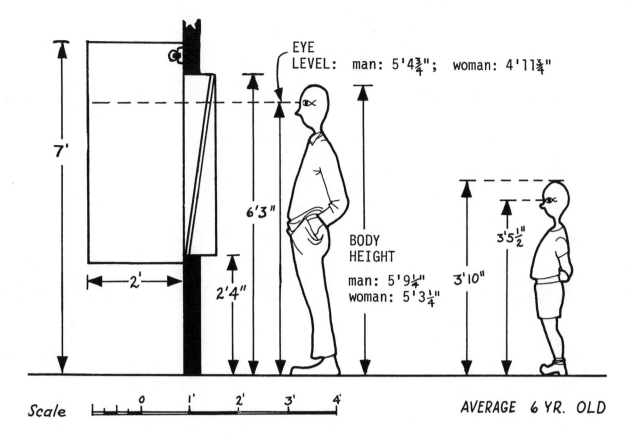

EYE LEVEL: man: 5'4¾"; woman: 4'11¾"

7'

6'3"

2'

2'4"

BODY HEIGHT
man: 5'9¼"
woman: 5'3¼"

3'10"

3'5½"

Scale 0 1' 2' 3' 4'

AVERAGE 6 YR. OLD

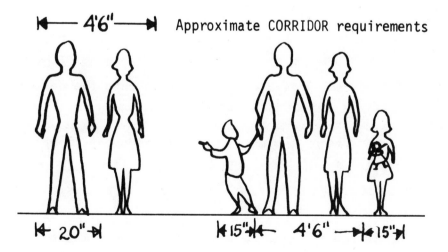

4'6" Approximate CORRIDOR requirements

20"

15" 4'6" 15"

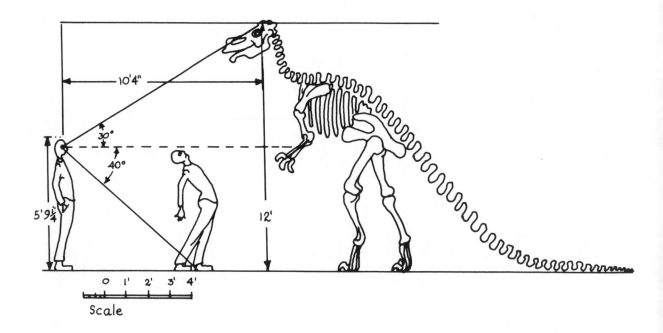

Some quite large objects, such as murals,
heroic statues, Greek friezes, totem poles or dino-
saurs, will inevitably soar above these viewing limits
and in this event, the visitor must be permitted space
to back far enough away from the object to comprehend
it without becoming a case for an orthopedic specialist.

Average body and eye-level heights for American
men and women and six-year-old children are shown on
the preceding page and are measurements the designer
should consider in basic exhibit planning.

One of the main things to remember about the
visitor is the short time-span he will devote to each
exhibit. Therefore, plan displays to emphasize those
main, basic, elemental facts you wish him to carry away.
It is equally important to remember that museum fatigue
is an ever-present problem, and places for the visitor
to sit down to rest *must* be *planned* as a part of the
regular traffic flow.

BUILDING MATERIALS AND DESIGN TECHNIQUES

The final factor in our planning list concerns a
knowledge of available cases and panels, and of building
materials and design techniques with which to build new
structures which the story presentation may require. An
inventory of display structures and lighting fixtures
already on hand but not in use should be made as soon as
the exhibit script and list of materials to be shown are
completed. Acquiring a knowledge of construction materials
will begin with "field" trips to the lumber yard, mill shops,
wrecking yards, sheet metal yards, hardware and building
supply stores. Wrecking yards are included for in these
one may find just the weathered wood, leaded windows,
elaborate mantlepieces, slabs of marble, intricate brass
hinges or some other item that will just exactly set off
a portion of a gallery. Wrecking yards are also an excellent source for well-aged framing lumber. Sheet metal
yards often will have remnant scraps of new materials --
aluminum extrusions, tubing, and sheet stock -- at reduced
prices. Surplus stores (those dealing in tools, radio parts,
aircraft surplus, nuts and bolts) may have just the gadget
that can be adapted to put motion or a changing light effect
into an exhibit. Businesses supplying display materials
for department stores will often have accessories that are
both useful and reasonably priced. Do not be startled, at
the end of August, to enter one of the stores and be surrounded by Christmas atmosphere. Seasonal items are stocked three
and four months in advance.

One of the best ways to build up an information file
about products is to write directly to the manufacturer. A
list of representative companies is included in the appendix.

A thorough knowledge of design factors comes through

training and experience, but the amateur can gain much by
a continual awareness of design elements used in every
visual medium. The alert museum preparator will find
himself looking at highway billboards, magazine editorial
and advertising layouts, television titles, department
store displays, travel agency windows, bank and financial
company exhibits, trade fairs, liquor-store and bar counter-
top displays, and any number of other places where good
design may be apparent, and thinking "how can I adapt
that to the museum?"

GALLERY DESIGN

Early museums which put study collections on display in the "visible storage" style previously discussed, often arranged the materials in broad categories and the display cases were placed in the galleries following a plan that is most reminiscent of book shelves in a library. This monotonous row-on-row layout survived to the present and frequently confronts museum visitors today.

In other museums, cases line the walls and the floor area is cluttered with unrelated left-over table cases and objects too large to be placed in the wall cases. "Confusion" best describes the "inspiration" for a room of this design.

The museum visitor is disoriented when he enters
the building. The monotony and/or clutter of these arrangements will do little to help him decide what he wants
to see first and which path to follow. Indeed, the first
appraisal of the room may create such visual fatigue
that the visitor may decide to by-pass the exhibits al-
together. If you have inherited a room arrangement
similar to these, and the cases cannot be moved without
being damaged, dismantle at least every other case and
remove it to create freer circulation for visitors and
provide areas for informational panels. However, with
the helpful advice of your local moving companies and

the aid of jacks and dollies, it is surprising how
many seemingly permanent installations can be re-
arranged. The re-installation should proceed as
finances and time become available.

Both photos this page courtesy of
New York State Museum, Albany, New York

Photo above is of same gallery as on page 39.

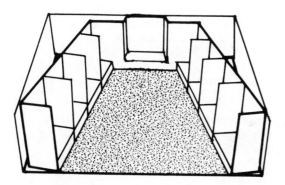

If nothing more is done than
to pull some cases from side walls,
tapering their lines to a far wall
so that the boxiness of the room
disappears, the gallery will become more inviting, and possibly
moving the cases around will
create space for storage or work
areas between them and the walls.

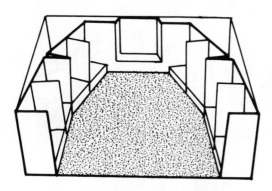

The flow of visitors is like the
flow of water in a stream. If the
cases are arranged with gently
curving lines to take advantage
of this pattern of movement,
visitors will find the room more
attractive and can progress easily
with the line of cases.

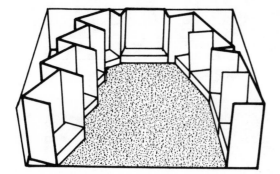

Often some of the cases can be
arranged in a staggered pattern
which produces a certain mystery
and a desire on the part of the
visitor to peek around corners
to see what is next.

It is not always necessary
to have a wide opening into
a hall. Cases that are arranged to narrow the entrance
a bit so that the hall inside then opens out, provide
a certain amount of interest.

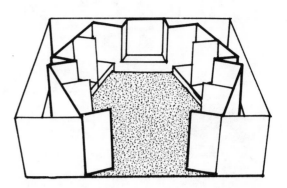

Working with the exhibit
script reveals logical
divisions in the story
and these help to deter-
mine alcove arrangements
of the cases. The al-
coves thus separate, by
actual physical divisions,
the various parts of
the story.

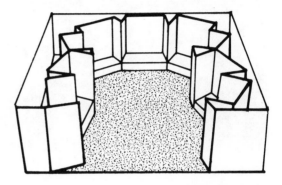

If the room is large enough,
some cases may be placed to
form an island creating a
more definite path in the
room interior.

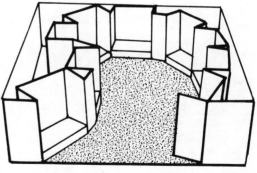

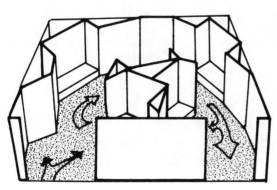

Nebraska State Historical Museum
                                 Lincoln, Nebraska

A capsule history
of the state pre-
sented immediately
inside the build-
ing entrance.

Attractive, well-
designed and well
executed "single-
topic" displays
permit the visitor
with little time
to gain a token
idea of Nebraska's
story.

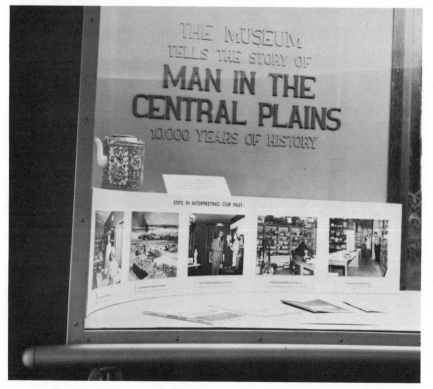

Visitors instinc-
tively grasp rail
installed just be-
low window area
instead of leaning
hands on glass.

Exhibit case is a continuous area divided by design elements rather than by physical barriers.

Maps, paintings, and photographic enlargements are among graphic devices used.

CORRIDORS

The physical proportions of corridors present
problems that are difficult but not impossible to solve.
It is most important to check with local building
authorities for safe and required minimum corridor widths
before starting to plan any hall-way exhibits.

MODELS of some suggested
treatments of corridors:

Scale: 1/2" = 1'

Typical 8' wide corridor
with 10' high ceiling;
picture molding at 7'
level.

Usual horizontal panel
installation emphasizes
length of hall, creates
monotony.

Addition of vertical
panels helps to break
up horizontal line.

VARIATIONS on the VERTICAL PANEL

Whenever a surface to be seen
is parallel to the visitor's
path, the visual material often
will be overlooked.

Placing the panel on a slight
angle with the wall helps to
interrupt the visual length
of the corridor. (4' wide panel
extends 2' on one side.)

reversible shelf

Glass top on shelf. Cut-outs
emphasize small objects

Shallow case

Both cases below extend 30"
into hall. Outer ends are
supported by spring-loaded
poles.

"See-through" specimen case
12" wide.

Shallow triangular case 48"
wide on panel tapering to
12" wide.

Corridor arrangement with
variation of panels and
accessories.

Architecture and the
Materials of Design

  Joslyn Art Museum
  Omaha, Nebraska

Note use of door
to help break
horizontal line
and to reinforce
architectural theme.

All measurements
are approximate.

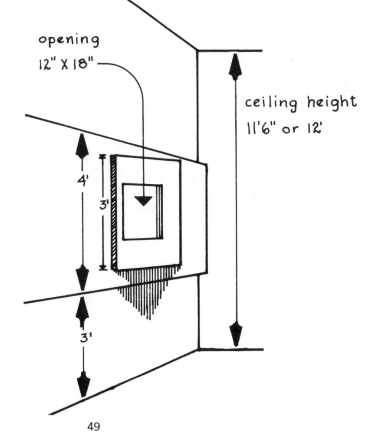

49

Designed for
the Farm

Joslyn Art Museum
Omaha, Nebraska

Angled wall case
and right-angle
panel isolate
and unify
material.

All measurements
are approximate.

ceiling height
11'6" or 12'

4'x8' panel

6'6" to
top of
wall case

Case is about
6" deep on near
side; 18" on far.

3'

3' 2'6"

6" baseboard

Hobby Hall   Carnegie Museum
                                    Pittsburgh, Pa.

Shallow wall cases with triangular space-dividers
provide an area for changing exhibits.

LIGHTING CORRIDOR EXHIBITS

A track lighting system may be installed along the
wall at the picture molding height to provide plug-ins
for shallow case exhibits. (See Lighting Manufacturers
listed in Appendix.)

Lighting may be adapted for panels by either of the
two following methods:

1. Existing corridor light.

   Glass shade and light bulb removed;
     replaced with screw-in swivel
     socket.

   Reflector flood or spot light screwed
     into swivel socket.

2. Wide corridors can be lighted by fluorescent lights
hidden behind a shield.

51

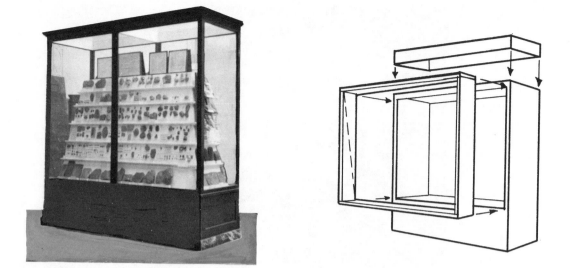

Simple open-top light "box" built of 1"x10" boards with two 1"x4" cross-supports and 4' fixture. Fixture is held 1 1/2" from wood supports by pipe nipple spacers (see Construction section).

Light cord may be held to under side of wood cross-supports and dropped down behind remodelled case.

BAFFLE for closed light box:

1" holes

bolt

Baffle of 1/4" masonite attached with 2 1/2" long 1/4" flat-head stove bolts, washers and nuts. Lengths of 3/8" inside diameter garden hose cut 1" long make spacers to hold baffle from side of light box. Hot air can escape but light is controlled.

masonite

52

EXHIBIT CASES

Often one is burdened with old cases equipped with glass doors, glass sides, and perhaps even a glass top. These glass surfaces pick up reflections from all over the room and from one another, making objects almost impossible to see. The case shown opposite can be remodelled in the following way.

Remove the glass doors and sides. Leave the glass top; the glass will filter ultraviolet rays of fluorescent lights, making it safer to display textiles or printed color. Build a light box to rest on top of the case. This will hold a four-foot fluorescent light fixture. If the light is too harsh in the case, smear the glass top with some Bon Ami. The dried cleanser will help to diffuse the light. A weak spotlight effect can be achieved by wiping the cleanser off in small circular areas, leaving clear glass "windows" surrounded by translucent cleanser-covered glass. A stronger spotlighting can be created by painting the top of the glass with ordinary household latex paint, leaving clear areas for the light to shine through. Do not fasten the light box to the case; let it rest on top so that replacing lights will be easy. A strip of weatherstripping of foam rubber glued around the bottom edge will help to prevent light from spilling out. The top of the box may be left open to contribute to the general room light, or may be closed to direct more light into the case interior. If the box is closed care should be taken to drill ventilation holes through the sides or top. An interior baffle will help to control spilling light.

Replace the glass of the back and sides of the case with quarter-inch or three-eighths-inch plyboard. If the glass is of good quality, free of ripples and many scratches, save it to be used on smaller cases that may be designed later. If it is not usable in the museum situation, try

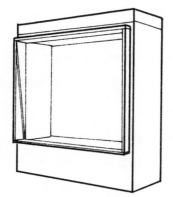

to sell it to a local salvage company.

Make a frame for the front of 1"x10" pine boards, fitting so it will just slide in the case. Push it in about four to six inches and fasten it securely. Screw strips of quarter-round molding to the frame for back stops for the glass. Set the strips so that the glass will be at the maximum slant possible with 10"-wide lumber. The slant will help to minimize reflections. Cut duplicate quarter-round for the front side of the glass. Set up the exhibit in the case, put in the glass, and screw the front set of molding strips to the frame. If the cases are to be arranged in alcoves, or if they are placed so that there is at least a four-foot working space between the case backs and the walls of the room, the plyboard backs may be made removable, so that it will not be necessary for the glass to be removed in order to change exhibits.

The larger case shown on the opposite page represents a different problem because of its size. The solution is similar but varies slightly.

Remove the glass from the sides. Remove the front doors and take out all shelving and shelf supports. Knock out the old flooring and build a new floor at least 24" from the floor of the room. If storage space is desired, cabinets may be built in under the floor. Build a frame for the glass similar to that shown with the previous case, but hold the frame at least fourteen inches from the top. Across the top, directly above the frame, make two hinged access panels to which fluorescent light fixtures will be attached. Opening

 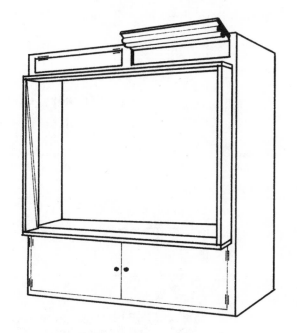

these panels makes it possible to change burned-out
lights without opening the case. Cover the visually
busy tongue-and-groove boards in the back with a
solid sheet of half-inch Cellotex or similar material.
Replacing the glass sides with three-eighths-inch
plyboard makes these side panels removable and gives
access to the case without having to remove the glass.

Remodeling of this typical old-style floor case

is very easy and can be done without having to disassemble anything but the interior.

(From a demonstration at the Adirondack Museum, Blue Mountain Lake, New York. Remodelling and case installation by H.J. Swinney, Director and George Bowditch, Exhibit Designer.)

Light box similar to that on page 52.

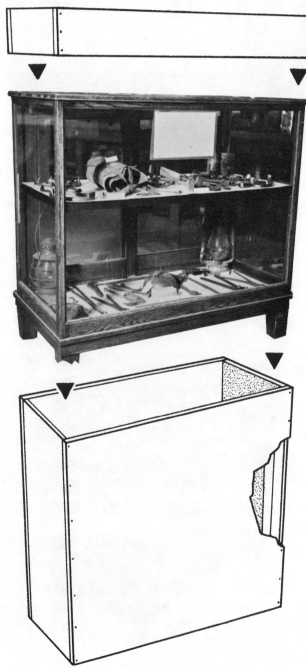

Base made of 1/2" plyboard reinforced at the corners with 2"x2" lumber.

Protruding edge of case rests on top of plyboard base. Weight holds pieces together. Light box rests on top of case.

Photo by George Bowditch

Before and After

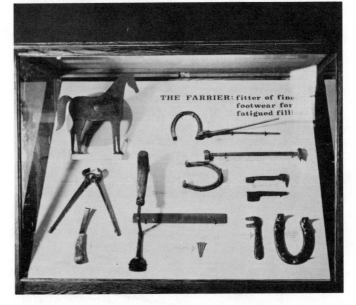

Sliding glass doors in back of case were
lifted out and shelf was removed. A tri-
angular box with selected tools attached to the front sloping
panel was slid into the exhibit case and the glass doors were
replaced. Excess materials were stored behind the sloping panel.
Had this been a permanent remodeling job rather

than a demonstration

the sliding glass doors
might have been painted or replaced with masonite.

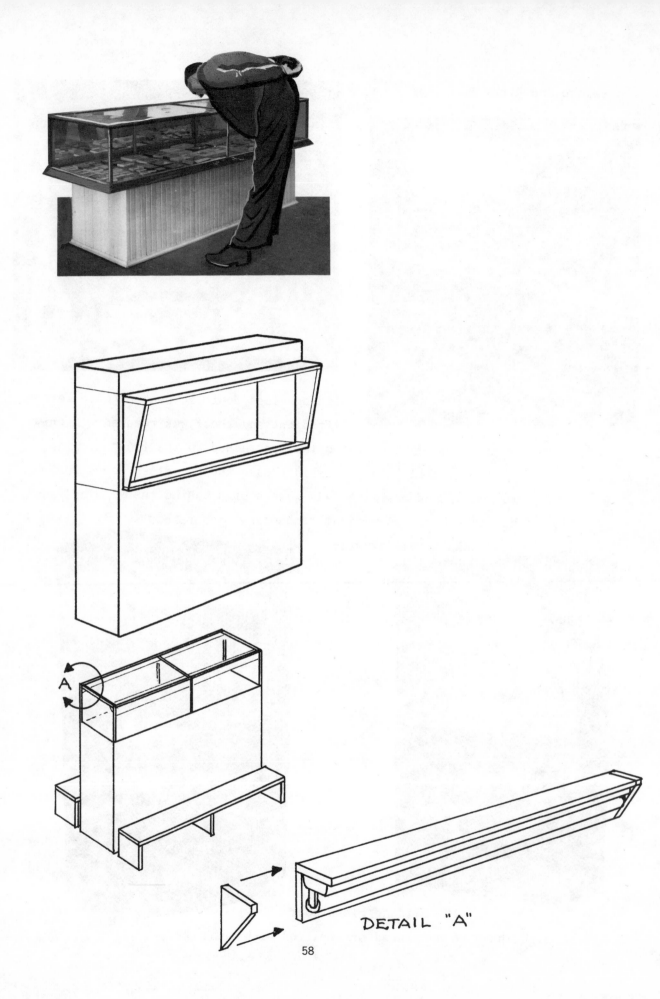

DETAIL "A"

58

Remodeling the case shown on the opposite page
proceeds as follows. Glass on one long side is replaced
by half-inch plyboard for a base, and the whole case is
tipped up on that side. The case is set on a new stand
at least forty inches high, and a light box is made, to
rest on top. The two short sides of glass are replaced
with plyboard, and a frame is made for the glass. The
sides of the frame are cut on the slant the glass will
follow. On this smaller case, the tapered cut keeps
the shadow-box frame from appearing top-heavy. The
contents of a case of the proportions shown would probably be viewed from a short distance, so it would not
be objectionable to use two pieces of glass for the
front, joining them with a strip of metal or wood molding.

An alternate method shows the case remaining a
floor display rather than being converted into a wall
case. The only changes are to raise the case so that the
base is at least forty inches high (again creating storage
space under the display area), and to make two light
troughs, each trough to hold two twenty-four-inch fluorescent fixtures, which are fastened inside the glass at the
top front and back edges of the case. The light cord extending from the base of the case may be placed on the
floor and covered with a protective metal strip. If
the material to be shown is such to be of interest to
children, an eight-inch high, eighteen-inch wide step
("riser") may be placed on each side.

When all the cases have been remodeled, they may
be distributed around a hall or gallery and a framework
of two-by-fours built between them to begin a continuous gallery wall.

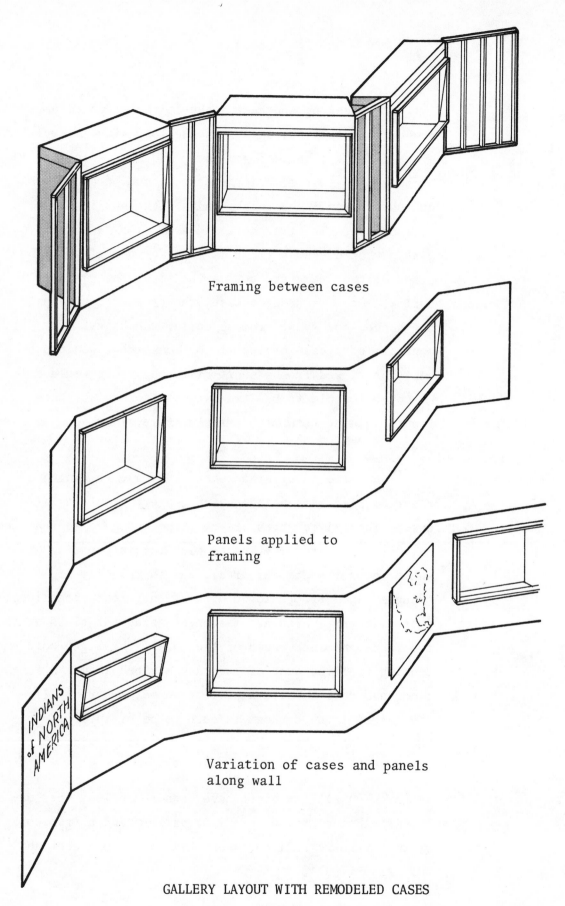

Framing between cases

Panels applied to framing

Variation of cases and panels along wall

INDIANS of NORTH AMERICA

GALLERY LAYOUT WITH REMODELED CASES

The two-by-four framing is covered with masonite, plyboard, plasterboard, Upson board or similar material, the joints and nail-holes are spackled and the wall is painted.

Individual cases with narrow connecting panels form an alcove in the Nebraska State Historical Museum.

Panel wall
with cases;
Red Men Hall
Museum,
Empire, Colo.

If the wall of the alcove is varied by the use of informational panels between some cases and the use of different size cases, such as those previously described, the room takes on more visual interest.

61

EXHIBIT CASES -- New construction

Simplified construction and the use of plyboard helps to hold down construction costs of new cases similar to those shown here. Designed by the author, these may be built by local contractors or ordered from CENTRAL DISPLAYS Inc., 1318 Tenth St., Denver, Colorado, 80204. Prices shown are for unpainted units and are effective as of October, 1968, F. O. B. Denver.

Free-standing <u>Large Panel Unit</u>: $125

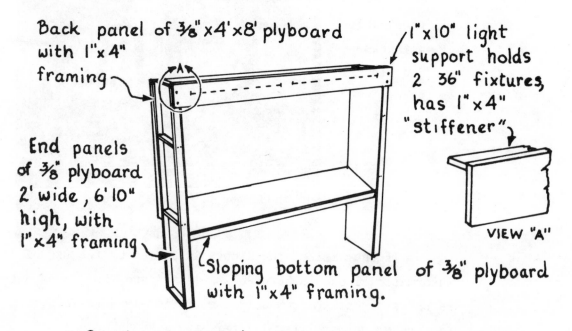

Back panel of ⅜"x4'x8' plyboard with 1"x4" framing

1"x10" light support holds 2 36" fixtures, has 1"x4" "stiffener"

End panels of ⅜" plyboard 2' wide, 6'10" high, with 1"x4" framing

VIEW "A"

Sloping bottom panel of ⅜" plyboard with 1"x4" framing.

Panels assembled with bolts and Tee-nuts.

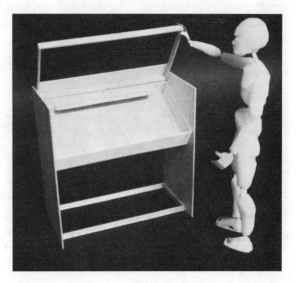

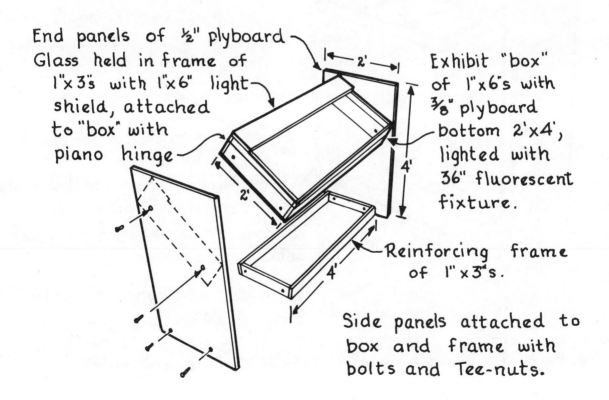

End panels of ½" plyboard
Glass held in frame of
1"x 3's with 1"x6" light
shield, attached
to "box" with
piano hinge

Exhibit "box"
of 1"x 6's with
⅜" plyboard
bottom 2'x4',
lighted with
36" fluorescent
fixture.

Reinforcing frame
of 1"x3"s.

Side panels attached to
box and frame with
bolts and Tee-nuts.

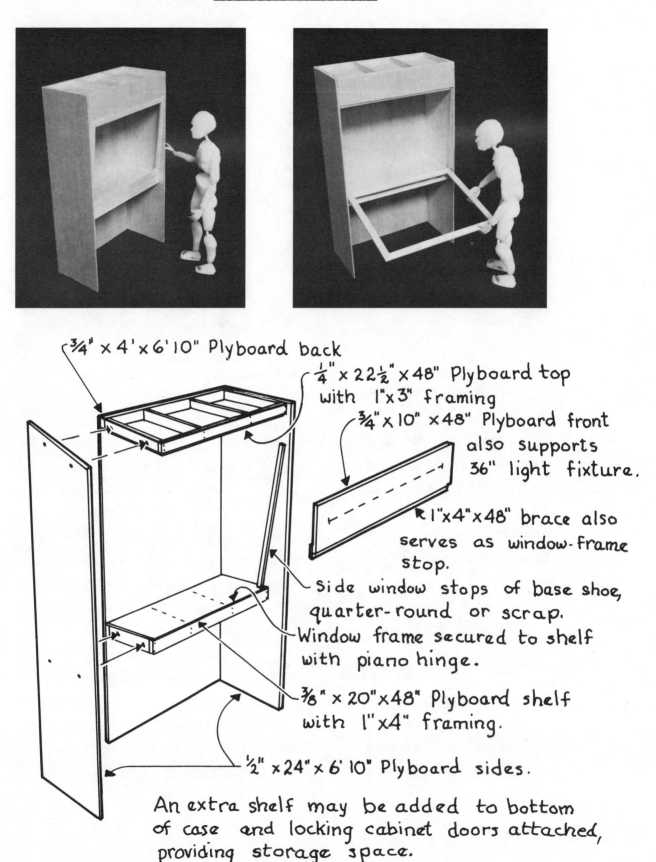

¾" × 4'× 6'10" Plyboard back

¼" × 22½" × 48" Plyboard top with 1"x 3" framing

¾" × 10" × 48" Plyboard front also supports 36" light fixture.

1"x 4"x 48" brace also serves as window-frame stop.

Side window stops of base shoe, quarter-round or scrap.

Window frame secured to shelf with piano hinge.

⅜" × 20"x 48" Plyboard shelf with 1"x 4" framing.

½" × 24"× 6' 10" Plyboard sides.

An extra shelf may be added to bottom of case and locking cabinet doors attached, providing storage space.

Free-standing <u>Exhibit Case</u>, 6' wide: $350

(Price includes dolly used to carry weight of
glass when case is opened.)

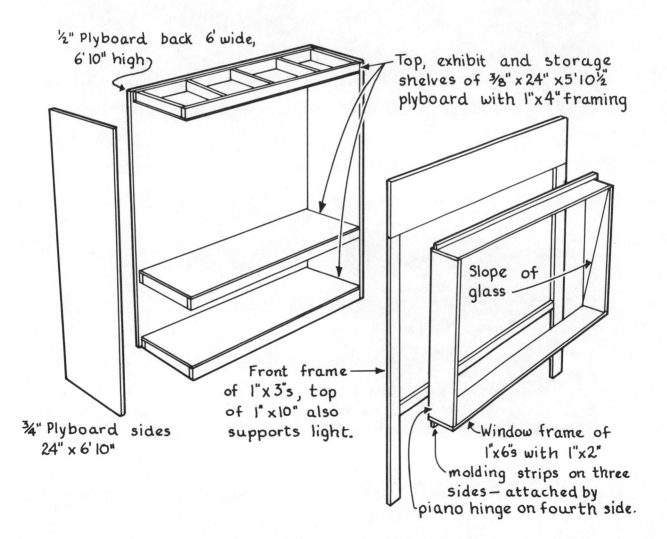

½" Plyboard back 6' wide,
6'10" high

Top, exhibit and storage
shelves of ⅜" x 24" x5'10½"
plyboard with 1"x4" framing

Slope of
glass

Front frame
of 1"x 3"s, top
of 1"x10" also
supports light.

¾" Plyboard sides
24" x 6'10"

Window frame of
1"x6"s with 1"x2"
molding strips on three
sides — attached by
piano hinge on fourth side.

Birds or linens --
this is visual monotony.

CASE EXHIBITS -- Designing the Setting

A case arranged with shelf after shelf of the same kind of object is just as monotonous and boring as the hall with row after row of cases. How the felony is compounded in a gallery where the row on row of cases are filled with shelf after shelf on which are displayed similar items, one after the other!

Try to avoid repetition.

Do not be afraid to avoid the boxiness of a case by putting in panels and false sides that angle from one side to the back. They can be used for main labels or for object display and are made of plyboard, Cellotex, Upson board or other panel material. Do not worry about mistakes in carpentry. Use Durham's Rock Hard Water Putty or Synkaloid Spackling Paste to fill the cracks. Be sure also to putty over the nail heads.

Hole cut in panel on left of case emphasizes pottery. Simple Cellotex boxes -- "case furniture"-- are used with the remaining materials.

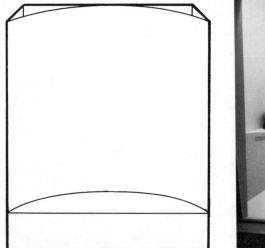 

A background panel which curves from side to side
or from top to bottom is made with one-eighth-inch Upson
board, called "Easy-Curve", which is available from lumber companies in sheets four feet by eight feet. A local
dealer who may not have Easy-Curve in stock can order it.

Panels may also slope from front to back. Use
half-inch Cellotex and support it underneath with braces
of one-inch by three-inch boards.

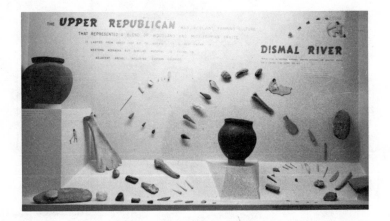

Often it is possible to combine sloping and angular panels or sloping and curved panels. Try many different arrangements. Try also not to repeat the same
pattern of display within one hall.

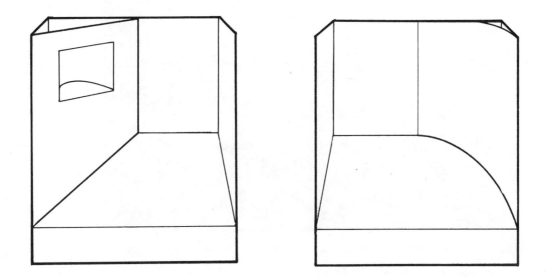

Combinations: Sloping and angular; sloping and curved.

Large corrugated cardboard cartons such as
those in which mattresses or pre-finished wooden
doors are packed may be obtained from furniture
stores or lumber dealers. The large sheets of
cardboard are used to cut preliminary patterns for
difficult fitting jobs.

Another variation is to cut a hole through the back of the case behind which a large artifact, photograph, or painting may be fastened.

The panel on the left which angles from the front of the case to the back, cutting across the corner, is made of plyboard to support the weight of a plaster replica of the Aztec calendar stone. The Easy-Curve background behind the effigy pot in the cut-out is curved from side to side. The artifact is lighted by a spotlight made from a two pound coffee can.

Remember constantly to use light, color, and texture in the designing of exhibits. Try a spotlight on some things. Use materials such as pegboard, fabric, sand-blasted or striated wood;

glue sand on some surfaces; try the effect of corrugated cardboard. Exercise your imagination. Try to counter one texture against another. For the hard surface of glass, metals, and minerals, try velvet cloth, flocked surfaces, or other soft textures.

A large scale model of the standard case will make it easier to visualize the design layout of panels and backgrounds and to estimate kinds and sizes of materials required.

CASE EXHIBITS -- Designing the Arrangement of Objects

Before a few of the design factors involved in arranging objects are described the problem of museum fatigue should be mentioned once more in its relation to the eye, to vision, and to comprehension. Convergence, by which our two eyes see as one, is brought about by two sets of muscles, six for each eye. Focusing is done by muscles attached to the lens. As with most muscles, fatigue will come to these eye muscles when they are held in the same position for some length of time. The muscles that, in focusing, contract or expand the lens will tire quickly if there is little or no variation in the depth of object placement within a case. The monotony and boredom of an almost constant focal depth produces a kind of hypnosis, but at the same time, there should not be a clutter of too many focal planes within the case.

Comprehension as well as vision must be at a high level for one to combat the ever-potential museum fatigue. This is comprehension of the object itself -- its shape, material, and size -- not the understanding of the identifying label. If, in an enthusiasm for

"atmosphere" and "psychological effect," case lighting
is not adequate, the effort to see and to comprehend
the materials on display cancels the attempted effective-
ness of the setting. Some factors that will bring on
visual and eventually full body fatigue are: monotony
in color, texture and light; straining to see without
adequate light; straining to see against improperly
directed light (such as a spotight in another area
of the gallery, daylight coming through windows,
multiple reflections of light in glass); and quantities of objects displayed with no regard for visual
selectivity and flow.

Each case should have one area (an object or
small group of objects) as a focal point. Then, as
the traffic flow in a gallery is directed in a pattern by the design and placement of cases and panels,
a visual flow within the case should pick up from
the focal area of interest and be established through
design factors such as emphasis (size and placement),
blank space, color, line, shape, texture, and light.
The use of these factors will help to accent, select,
set apart, or consolidate information. A typical
display problem is that of a number of objects which
differ perhaps only in minor details -- prehistoric
pottery, mineral specimens, guns, or a series of
clocks. Making the most appealing, interesting, sig-
nificant, or important specimen a key attraction and
using one or a combination of design factors attracts
the eye to that key specimen and will lead it to
the others.

Wherever possible, all materials should be
shown in the same position as they were when used,
helping the visitor to visualize the function.

72

DESIGN FACTORS USED IN ARRANGEMENT OF OBJECTS

Emphasis through size (of case furniture) and place-ment;

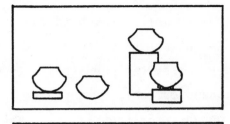

Emphasis through isolation;

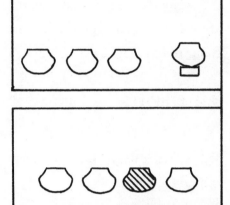

Emphasis through color (if specimens permit);

Emphasis through line, size and placement;

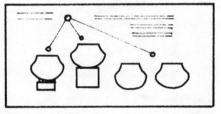

Emphasis through shape (by color or overlay of differ-ent material);

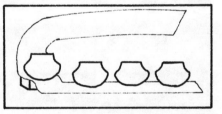

Emphasis through texture;

Emphasis through light, size and placement.

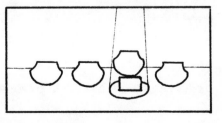

73

One approach to the problem of designing the layout is to set the objects in the case, working with stacks of books, two-pound coffee cans, boards, cigar boxes, cardboard cartons, or anything that will give the desired height. By experimenting with the boxes and objects, considering the size and location of case labels, one arrives at a final design that attracts and focuses attention, then leads logically through the case.

CASE EXHIBITS -- "Furniture"

The term "case furniture" refers to the boxes, pedestals and other structures used to support the exhibit specimens.

They may be simple rectangular forms or more elaborate constructions.

After the case layout has been determined (as described above), measure how high, wide, and deep the boxes for case furniture must be. Make the boxes from pieces of one-half-inch Cellotex, three-eights-inch Upson board, or, for heavy specimens, one-quarter-inch or three-eighths-inch plyboard. Pieces are fastened

together with Elmer's
glue or Weldwood glue
(the powdered plastic
resin that is mixed
with water as needed)
and tacked with finish-
ing nails which are
set just below the
surface. Raw edges
are filled with spackl-
ing paste which is sanded
lightly when it has dried.

Ordinary rubber-based (latex) house-interior paints are used
for painting both the case and the boxes at the same time, so
that they will match. In most case designs, it is better
that this "furniture" match the case interior so that the
objects displayed on the boxes, through their contrasting
color, assume more importance than their supports. The

"architecture" of an exhibit (the structures that hold the
items in place) should never become so interesting in itself,
or so dominant, that the exhibit materials are lost in a maze.

PANELS

The use of panels in corridors already has been discussed. Panels have additional uses in exhibit rooms as
well where they may serve as directional devices, as supports for information, or may form a free-standing wall.

It is not necessary that panels be a single, flat
plane. They acquire more visual interest if they combine
two or more planes, have additional areas added to their
surfaces, or have small exhibit cases fastened on the front
or behind framed openings.

These photographs and sketches show only a few of
the many variations of panel uses one may design.

Curved plyboard panel provides area for
information and acts as a directional
device in exhibit at the University
Museum, University of Pennsylvania,
Philadelphia, Pennsylvania.

Spring-loaded poles support light-weight panels at the St. Louis Academy of Science, St. Louis, Mo.

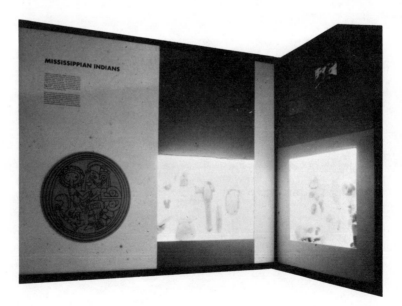

Shallow, lighted exhibit boxes mounted on back of panels display selected artifacts.

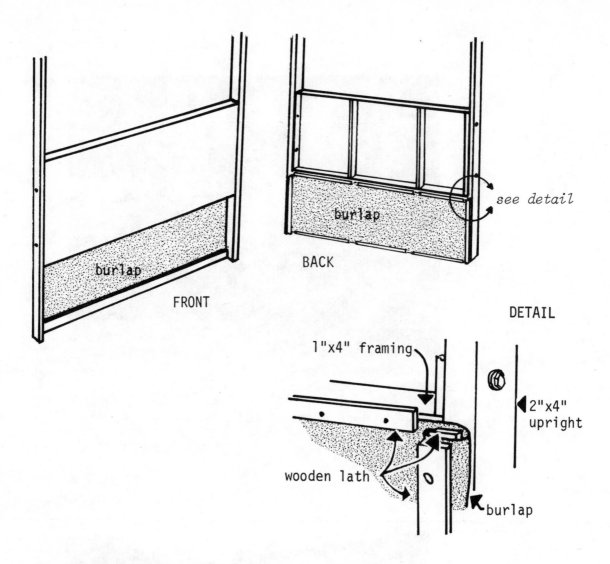

FRONT

BACK

see detail

DETAIL

1"x4" framing

2"x4" upright

wooden lath

burlap

burlap

burlap

Simple panel of 3/16" x 4'x8' Upson board glued and
nailed to 1"x4" framing; bolted to two 2"x4"s which
are capped by spring-loaded units (Brewster's "Timber Toppers") to hold in vertical position.

Colored burlap stretched across bottom is held in
place with wooden laths.

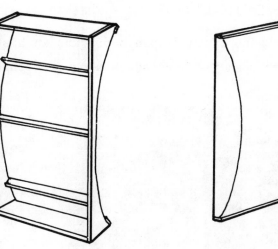

1/8" sheet of 4'x8' Easy-Curve mounted on curving
supports cut from 1"x10" shelving with additional
1"x4" bracing on back. Reverse curve is constructed
from pieces cut from one-by-tens (for left panel)
and an additional sheet of Easy-Curve. Bracing in
back is similar.

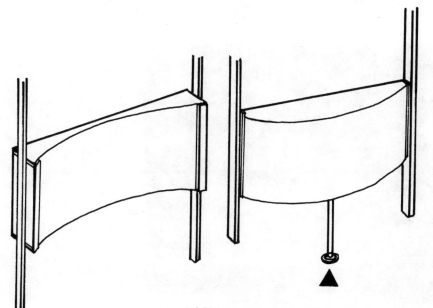

Additional support made of 3/4" pipe. Floor
flanges fasten pipe to panel bottom framing
and to plyboard disc which rests on floor.

"PROBLEMATICAL" OBJECTS -- What to do with a gun collection

Too often displays of guns in historical museums resemble an illustrated catalogue in three dimensions.

Only gun-lovers could find these two exhibits of interest -- and they would have difficulty seeing details of the exhibited specimens!

Gun Exhibit, New Illinois
State Museum, Springfield,
Illinois

When the Illinois State
Museum acquired a new
building, their old gun
display (lower picture,
opposite page) was dis-
carded for a completely
new approach.

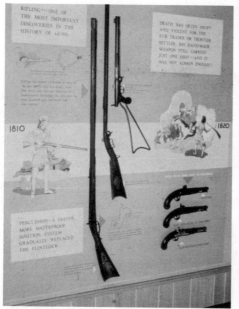

The new gun exhibit is one of
the best this writer has seen.
The important developments in
firearms are tied in with the
history of the country by the
use of a continuous time-line
and key illustrations.

The resulting exhibit is
of interest to many people
who might otherwise find a
gun display dull.

Duplicate guns have been
retired to an available
study collection.

"PROBLEMATICAL" OBJECTS -- What to do with old farm implements

Without some kind of organization and interpretation old farm implements have little meaning for today's young people.

An approach to understanding is provided if no more is done than to group tools with similar functions together on common panels. (One might wish the labels had been printed on less conspicuous paper.)

Photo courtesy of Kansas State Historical Museum, Topeka, Kansas

Use of textured wood and massive vertical supports (suggesting barn construction) is pleasant and appropriate.

Placing the implements in a stylized farm setting conveys an immediate impression as to general
function. The platform serves a double purpose: it
raises the machinery and tools to a more accessible
viewing height and discourages the visitor from step-
ping into the exhibit area. A layer of gravel on the
platform surface is visually pleasing and has the advantage of showing little dust and dirt.

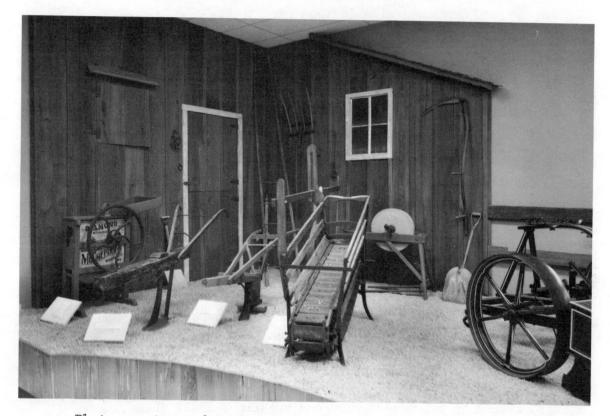

Photo courtesy of Kansas State Historical Museum, Topeka, Kansas

At the Farmers' Museum in Cooperstown, New York, rural
implements of the early nineteenth century are arranged
according to "The Farmer's Year." For each section a
large panel provides an introduction with the name of
the month and a headline label. Appropriate equipment
for the season is shown with samples of crops, printed

advertisements and other associated items. One section
label reads:

JULY

Hay-making

Hay was formerly one of the chief crops
of our state. Timothy and clover were grown
to feed the thousands of horses on the farms
and towpaths, turnpikes and towns.

Everyone available took part in hay-
making. It was usually cut and left to cure,
then piled up in large stacks or put into
barns. In poor hay years the animals would
winter on corn stalks or grainstraw, or else
the farmer was obliged to butcher them.

"PROBLEMATICAL" OBJECTS -- Period rooms

Period rooms, which are constructed to re-create
the feeling of a particular historic time, often are
presented in a series similar to the street window displays of department stores or full-scale versions of a
one-story doll house. They are used best when they are
incorporated with a variety of other visual techniques
as a working part of a larger story. Panels and cases
on each side of the period room can highlight small items,
giving the visitor an opportunity for closer scrutiny
while associating the objects both with the time period
and the specific room.

The log house interior shown at the top of the opposite page, is placed across the end of a corridor in the
permanent exhibit "Life on the Prairie" at the Joslyn Art
Museum, Omaha, Nebraska.

Sometimes the same emotional response may be evoked by a simple layout in a shallow case. Full background paintings with related objects dramatize the back-breaking chores of a pioneer housewife in these two exhibits in the Nebraska State Historical Museum, Lincoln, Nebraska.

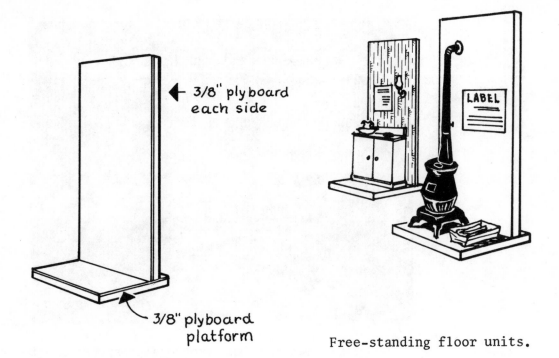

← 3/8" plyboard
each side

3/8" plyboard
platform

Free-standing floor units.

1"x 4" framing

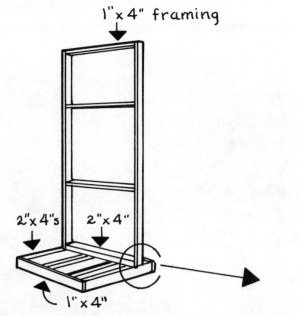

2"x 4"s   2"x 4"

1"x 4"

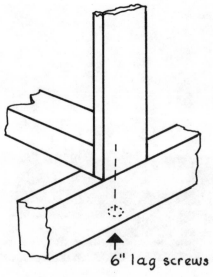

6" lag screws

Panel and platform combinations may be used to present large, heavy, or bulky objects and, by use of appropriate wall-paper and other accessory items, can provide an inexpensive but effective approach to the period room concept.

The units shown on the opposite page may be distributed as "island" units in a room. Fully finished, the backs provide areas for display of flat visuals -- maps, photographs, and paintings -- while the fronts create space for large objects. The units are useful for exhibits of heavy machinery such as early farm equipment or engines as well as for furniture.

The wall and platform combination shown above functions well at the Illinois State Museum in Springfield. Primitive American paintings shown with contemporary arts and crafts create a definite mood and feeling for pioneer times.

COLOR and LIGHT

Color and light are two design factors which, though inexpensive, can enhance any display when used with imagination and discrimination.

Choice of color starts with the theme and the objects that are to be used in conveying that theme. Gallery or hall walls, floor and ceiling may be considered a "background" for the presentation and should complement, not compete with, the specimens on view. Some very general considerations regarding color are listed below.

Gallery wall colors can suggest a natural environment or an architectural period. Examples seen have been:

> light and dark grey stains on textured wood used in a mining exhibit in an historical museum;
>
> "barn" red used with farm machinery;
>
> pale blue used in a room exhibiting Eskimo artifacts;
>
> clear yellow walls in a room of Plains Indian materials;
>
> very dark green behind Iroquois false faces (which were suspended by nylon fishing line, lighted by concealed spots);
>
> sandy buff in an Egyptian hall;
>
> aqua blue (more a blue than turquoise) in a gallery of classic Mediterranean cultures;
>
> deep purple, white and gray with exhibits of Medieval armor.

Varying shades of the same basic color may be used

to unify different aspects of a general subject; e.g., a light blue background might be used for pre-Civil War military exhibits and a darker blue for cavalry displays of the Indian wars period. Both subdivisions might have several case exhibits but the unifying wall color would tie them together visually and psychologically.

Color can help visually to change the size and shape of a room. Dark walls will tend to shrink a huge room; light ones will expand a small one. A dark wall at the end of a long, narrow room will give the impression of shortening and widening that room.

If the ceiling of a room is cluttered with pipes or unsightly beams, a dark color -- even a flat or satin-finish black -- will make the pipes and angles of the beams virtually disappear. A light-colored ceiling will add visually to the height of the room. In a hall exhibiting birds, walls were painted varying shades of beige (according to land areas occupied by the birds shown) and the ceiling was painted a sky blue. Coves above the case walls provided an indirect source of light for the ceiling which appeared much higher than its actual height.

Specific case colors should be chosen in relation to the objects displayed in the cases. A dark-colored case will make light-colored materials appear larger than they are by the contrast; a light-colored case will make dark materials look smaller.

If in doubt, use of a background complementary color (those shown on opposite sides of a color wheel) is usually safe.

Certain colors (hues of red, orange and yellow)

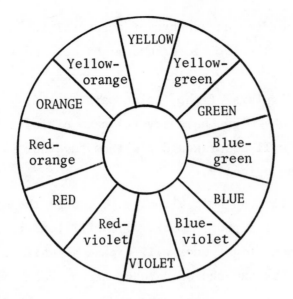

seem "warm" and tend, visually, to advance while others
(the various blues) appear "cool" and seem to retreat.
Green and violet hues are half-way between warm and
cool, and vary in their tendency to "advance" or "retreat"
according to the proportion of warm or cool colors they
contain.

When colors for the gallery walls and cases have
been chosen, a few accent colors may be used on the three-
dimensional letters of the headline label or sparingly to
attract attention to key parts of the installation. Care
should be taken, however, not to combine too many colors
nor to use too many "accents" in a single display. As
with gallery planning or case layout, simplicity is more
successful than complexity.

Many paint companies maintain a staff interior
decorator whose advice may be free. If in doubt it is
wise to seek this professional help.

LIGHT

Controlled light can do much to create a mood,
change visual pace, indicate an historic period or a
natural environment, and can aid in visitor circulation through the use of proper placement and direction.
Daylight, streaming in through windows, is uncontrolled
and may vary from dazzling brightness on a sunny day to
a dull, flat grayness when the weather is overcast.
Ideally, museum *exhibit areas* should be windowless,
permitting complete control with artificial light.

In old buildings which are lined with windows,
exhibit rooms may be improved by painting the windows
to block out the light. If the gallery is planned with
false walls which are placed at least four or five feet
away from the room wall, light from the windows will
be effectively shielded and diffused.

Both fluorescent and incandescent lights may be
used (sometimes in combination) to good advantage. Most
rooms will receive enough illumination from lights inside
the display cases. Where large wall areas are to be
lighted evenly (as in a picture gallery or wall-panel
arrangement) fluorescent lights mounted in a cove or
wall bracket provide a "wash" of light. (See Construction section for details of wiring and installation.)
Fluorescent lighting is economical, providing almost
three times as much light as incandescent for the same
power consumption. It yields a "soft" diffused light
which minimizes shadows and burns with less heat than
incandescent.

"Deluxe Cool-White" fluorescent lamps make colors
appear almost as they would in daylight; "Deluxe Warm-
White" lamps provide a "warm" light approaching the color
of incandescent lamps which emphasize reds, oranges and
yellows. Great care should be taken in the selection

91

of fluorescent lamps in order to get the best color
rendition and, once a definite lamp has been chosen,
the effort must be made to replace burned-out lamps
with exactly the same type in order to maintain the
original color effect. It is wise to plan and paint
gallery walls and case interiors under the same
lighting conditions as will be operating regularly.

The following chart shows some of the color
changes which may be anticipated with various lamps:

Painted color	Incandescent	Fluorescent		
		Standard Cool-White	Deluxe Cool-White	Deluxe Warm-White
Light yellow	Vivid yellow-orange	Bright yellow	Bright yellow	Deep yellow
Medium blue	Blue-green	Gray-blue	Reddish-blue	Purple-blue
Cherry red	Bright red-orange	Yellow-red	Cherry red	Orange-red

Fading of displayed material is another factor to
consider in use and placement of light. Fluorescent
lamps should be at least twelve inches from the front
surface of any fabrics, paintings, or color-printed
pages. Translucent plastic tubes (known as ultraviolet, or UV sleeves) may be slipped over fluorescent
lamps to help reduce fading.

Incandescent lights provide sparkle and color
in exhibits of gems, jewelry and cut crystal. Specific
highlighting of large floor displays such as sculpture,
historic vehicles, and machinery may be accomplished
with the use of reflector spots and floodlights. The
Swivelier Company, Inc. manufactures a porcelain

swivel-socket which may be screwed into an existing
porcelain socket to provide a heat-resistant, directional device for reflector spots and floods.

The combination of a fluorescent lamp for
general lighting with emphasis on a key specimen
provided by a low (75 watt) wattage reflector spot
may be used inside some case exhibits. Care must
be taken to provide for adequate ventilation and
air circulation whenever incandescent lights are
used within a case.

General illumination from an overhead
fluorescent light.

Many different display lighting fixtures
and systems are available to the exhibit designer.
A partial list of manufacturers is given in the
Appendix.

General overhead illumination plus hard
side light.

Hard side light with less
overhead light   creates
shadow and more dramatic
effect.

Diffused side light deepens
mood but lessens comprehension of object.

LABELS

A label is a sign. It informs; it explains; sometimes, it directs. It is not, and should not pretend to be, a book. It should be concise and written in simple, direct, uncomplicated, and unpretentious language. Because labels usually will be read by standing people, and because most people are not physically conditioned for this, the important part of the label should be at the beginning.

If labels are arranged like a newspaper's headlines and stories, many visitors will read them. Some people read only the headlines. Some read headlines and subheads. Still others read everything, including the classified ads and obituaries. Labels can be designed to satisfy all groups.

A well-designed gallery will be arranged in a sequence so that each display is a part of a continuous story. Logically, in such a gallery there will be the following labels:

1. A large sign placed at or near the entrance which informs the visitor of the contents of the room. If, for example, the area is full of old glass, the "room label" or "gallery label" permits those people for whom old glass holds no attraction to save their feet and eye muscles for exhibits in which they *do* have an interest. Letters forming this label may be three-dimensional and should be at least four inches high.

2. Each case or panel exhibit will have a large "headline" label which will serve the same function as the headline of a newspaper. It will attract attention, focus interest on the case, and will be short and to the point. To be read easily,

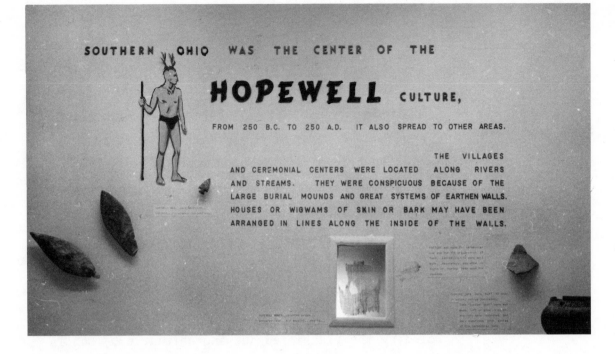

SOUTHERN OHIO WAS THE CENTER OF THE

HOPEWELL CULTURE,

FROM 250 B.C. TO 250 A.D. IT ALSO SPREAD TO OTHER AREAS.

THE VILLAGES AND CEREMONIAL CENTERS WERE LOCATED ALONG RIVERS AND STREAMS. THEY WERE CONSPICUOUS BECAUSE OF THE LARGE BURIAL MOUNDS AND GREAT SYSTEMS OF EARTHEN WALLS. HOUSES OR WIGWAMS OF SKIN OR BARK MAY HAVE BEEN ARRANGED IN LINES ALONG THE INSIDE OF THE WALLS.

it may be the main phrase, emphasized by size, in an introductory sentence (as shown above). These headline labels should be written in such a manner that the visitor who reads only these labels may still gain a narrative account of the total story told by the exhibits in the hall. The headline label is usually made up of three-dimensional letters of two sizes.

3. Secondary labels follow the headline and take the function of the sub-head of a newspaper, containing a little more detail and expanding the information. These letters usually are also three-dimensional but are a smaller size than letters used in the sentence and main phrase of the headline label (also illustrated above).

4. Specimen labels, which go with each object on view, then continue the story in detail. The leading sentence in the specimen label should be a topic sentence (which may be emphasized by using bolder

type or a three-dimensional letter), and the rest of the paragraph should explain further the statements contained in that sentence. Where several objects are similar, a long label can be written, then divided, and some portion of it put with each object. The topic sentence of this long label should serve to group the objects together under one general heading within the case. As an example, in a display that included many kinds of old bottles, a topic sentence might read:

> "It is sometimes possible to date the occupancy of an abandoned house by the kinds of glass fragments found within it."

The remainder of the label could explain early methods of manufacture and how they can be recognized, and the items of glass would serve as illustrations to the label. The long label would be physically divided (cut apart) and a portion placed with each appropriate object. Visitors are invariably more interested in *what* a thing is, *who* made it, *where, when, how* and *why* it was used, than they are in the fact that Joe Smith gave it to the museum in 1928 and that it originally cost him ten dollars.

It is regrettable that many art museums continue simply to hang their permanent collections of prints and pictures on their walls and to display their sculptures on floor stands accompanied only by labels that name the artists, the dates when they lived, and the name of the donor. How much more effective would be art exhibitions that included introductory labels to explain the basic facts of various art movements and transitional labels to show their development. The attempt to place artists and their various "schools"

97

within a frame of reference understandable to the untrained
layman might result in support for the art museums' programs
coming from totally unexpected sources!

When laying out titles and text, it is very easy to

become so interested in the design of the total letter and
word area that an interesting pattern which uses the words
as decoration may result. This does not necessarily mean
that the words themselves are easy to read. When words
are split up and used as decoration, or are arranged at
odd angles in a mistaken striving for "effect," they are
awkward to read and their meaning becomes difficult to
grasp. Use of tricky, cute, or unusual type is never
justified if it is being used *only* for the sake of being
different. If an unusual type face really helps to communicate -- fine. Otherwise, remember that your labels
are designed with just one purpose in mind. You want
people to read them.

It is a good idea, once one or two type faces have
been chosen for a particular gallery, to use them consis-
tently without adding more styles. Too many styles within

a given area will prove distracting.

The best label is one which is so well written, arranged, and lettered that it leaves the visitor almost unaware of technique and able to concentrate on the meaning of the words.

Instructions for making three-dimensional alphabets, hand-lettering, the use of stencils, "Instant" type (dry transfer letters) and other labelling techniques are given in the Construction Methods Section.

Part II:

CONSTRUCTION NOTES

INTRODUCTION

Many museum presentations may be constructed
by the dedicated volunteer who is a week-end carpenter. Often, these constructions may serve the small
museum better than the expensive commercial units that
are available. Some ideas on construction are presented in this section.

Perhaps more than anything else in construction,
the museum exhibit builder should consider *ease of
maintenance*. No exhibit will remain fresh-looking
forever. How lights are to be changed, colors touched
up, and out-of-date labels replaced should be major
factors in any design.

TOOLS

Buy the best quality made.
TAKE PROPER CARE OF THEM.

Basic Hand Tools

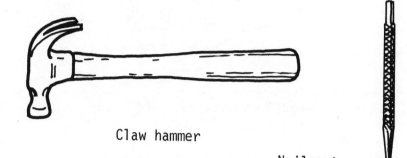

Claw hammer

Nail set

Claw Hammer

A bell-faced hammer has a slightly rounded face
and is recommended as a beginning tool because a nail
can be driven flush with the wood without leaving hammer dents. Buy one made of drop-forged tempered steel.
Cast heads may chip or break and are dangerous to use.
Handles are usually of hickory, steel, or fiberglass,
all of which are recommended. Two weights (which refers to the weight of the hammer head) are useful: the
16 ounce is used for heavy-duty, all-purpose hammering;
the 10 ounce for lighter, more delicate work.

A few working tips:

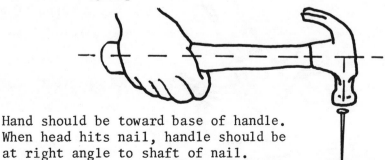

Hand should be toward base of handle.
When head hits nail, handle should be
at right angle to shaft of nail.

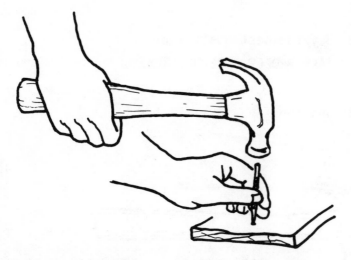

Nail set should be used with *all* brads
and finishing nails. Spackling paste
is used to fill the hole before the wood
is painted. Plastic wood may be used if
the surface is to be stained.

A piece of light weight cardboard
(such as shirt cardboard from the laundry)
is used to start a small nail. Push the
nail through the cardboard. Hold the
cardboard and, when the nail is driven
almost flush, tear cardboard away before
the final blows are delivered.

Before trying to drive a small nail
through hardboard, such as Masonite, drill
a small hole. (Clip the head off a small
nail of the same size you intend to use,
and use this nail for the drill.)

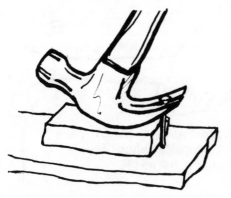

Slip a scrap of wood under
the claws of the hammer to
increase leverage and to
help prevent damage to the
wood surface when pulling
out a nail.

Hand Crosscut Saw

Saws are measured by length and by the number

of teeth (called "points") in an inch. The number of
points is usually marked on the blade. A 24 inch, 10
point saw is a good general-purpose size.

Marks of a good saw: it should be flexible,
the blade made of tempered spring steel so it may be
filed and sharpened; the edge with the teeth should
be thicker than the back to provide firmness at the
cutting edge and clearance for the rest of the saw
in the "slot" (called a "kerf") being cut; the blade
surface should be ground and polished and the handle
should be made of hardwood fastened with brass rivets.

A few working tips:

Use the knuckle of your
thumb to guide the saw
when starting the cut.

Remember the saw has a
thickness and cut on the
waste side of a measured
line.

waste

107

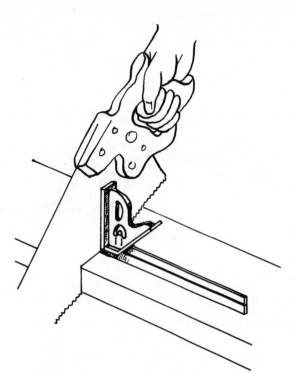

Use a combination square to insure a true right-angle cut.

A long 2x4 board which is straight and has true right-angle sides is clamped with C-clamps along a line to make accurate long cuts from plyboard sheets. Slip scrap cardboard between the jaws of the clamps and the plyboard surface to protect the wood.

A thin edge may be trimmed from the end of a board by clamping waste stock to the board and sawing through both pieces. Protect the good stock from clamp dents by using scrap cardboard between the clamp head and the board surface.

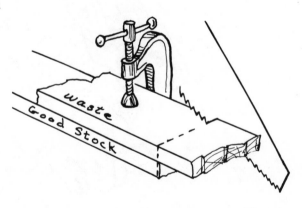

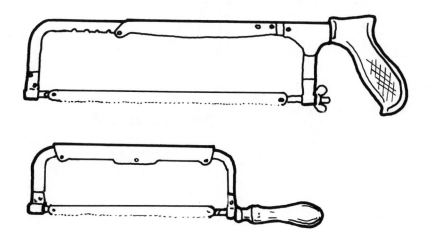

    Hack saws are used to cut metal such as steel
and aluminum angle-iron and bars, aluminum tubing,
pipe or conduit, and to trim bolts. Two styles are
shown: a wing-nut tightens blade tension on the
heavy-duty saw above; the handle tightens the blade
on the saw below. Blades are inserted with the teeth
pointing away from the handle and a blade with 18
teeth per inch is best for general use. A blade with
32 teeth per inch is used for thin material.

    Starting the cut is easier if a nick is made
in the metal surface with a file.

    Clamp a thin sheet of metal between two pieces
of wood (in a vise or with C-clamps) to saw without
bending the metal and to get a clean cut.

    Thread a nut onto a bolt before sawing the bolt
to correct length. The nut may be held in a vise and,
when the cut has been made, the nut cleans the bolt
threads as it is removed.

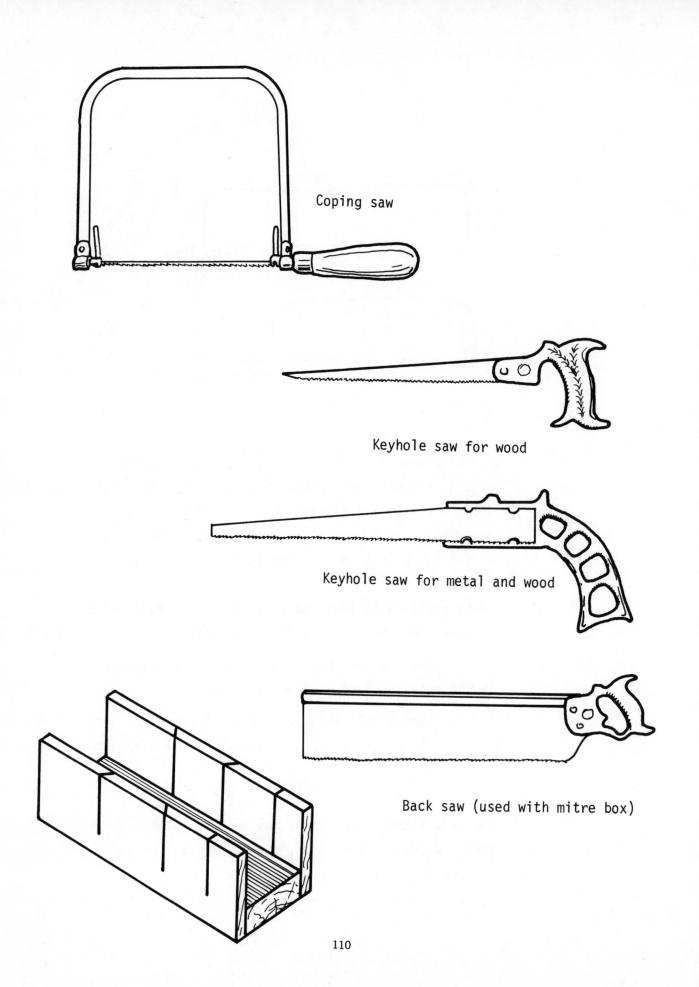

Coping saw

Keyhole saw for wood

Keyhole saw for metal and wood

Back saw (used with mitre box)

110

Coping Saws are used to cut intricate, irregular and curved shapes in thin wood, hardboard, cardboard, plastic and sheet metal. Blades have pins through each end which catch in slots, and are mounted in the frame with teeth pointing toward the handle. Tension is maintained by tightening the handle and most saws are adjustable so that the blade may be rotated in the frame. Many blades are available, from those with 8 teeth per inch and about 1/8 inch wide, to those with 32 teeth per inch and less than 1/16 inch wide. A spiral blade is also on the market, which makes it unneccessary to change blade direction while cutting. Heavy, coarse blades are used with wood and plastic; fine, thin blades work well with cardboard (several layers of which may be stapled together for multiple copies), hardboard and metal. (See use of coping saw in section on making three-dimensional alphabet letters.)

Keyhole Saws can be used to cut gently curving lines in plyboard; to cut out large holes in the middle of plyboard sheets; to cut openings for pipes and electrical outlets. The narrow, tapered blade can cut in places where other saws cannot be used. Some types come with interchangeable blades.

A Back Saw is used with a miter box to cut moldings for glass, case opening trim, frames for prints, photographs, etc. The reinforced back provides rigidity and the blade, which can range from 10 to 12 inches in length, may have 10 to 14 teeth per inch. A useful size is 12 inches long with 14 teeth per inch.

Inexpensive wooden miter boxes may be purchased with slots for 90° and 45° cuts.

Screwdrivers are probably the most abused tools in any tool-kit. They should never be used as chisels, paint-can openers or pries. They should be used *only* for driving screws. Buy good ones with handles large enough to grip. A basic set would include: a No. 2 with a 1/4-inch blade, No. 3 with a 5/16-inch blade, and a No. 4 with a 3/8-inch blade. Adding one small and one medium size Phillips screwdriver for Phillips-head screws (with a cross instead of a straight slot) and a Z-shaped offset screwdriver for

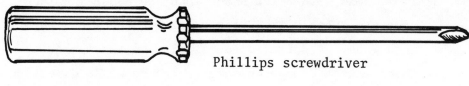

Phillips screwdriver

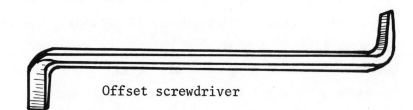

Offset screwdriver

work in close quarters will complete a "first" list of necessary screwdrivers.

Always use a screwtip that *fits the slot* of the screw. An oversize tip will chew up surrounding wood when the screw is forced in; an undersize tip will not distribute enough force to turn the screw and will become rounded when it slips out of the screw slot. The screw tip should completely fill the slot and should *not* be rounded or beveled.

A small hole should be pre-drilled into the material before the screw is driven to avoid splitting the wood. If a screw is hard to drive, try coating the threads with soap. If it is still difficult to turn, back it out and enlarge the pilot hole. Forcing it may break it off in the hole.

Pliers

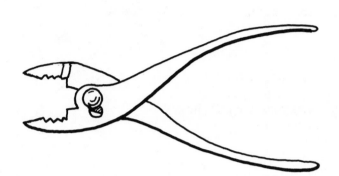

Pliers (with jaws slipped
for wider grip)

Pliers

Round-nose, slip-jawed pliers are most common
and are used in a variety of holding jobs. Fine
grooves at the rounded tip hold small objects, larger
grooves farther back hold nuts and bolts and round
objects (pipe or tubing). To grasp larger objects
slip jaws wide until the pivot bolt slides into other
hole.

The grooves of all pliers should be kept clean.

Other useful pliers include:

Combination pliers --
a heavy squared nose
combined with wire-
cutting action;

Narrow-nosed -- helps to
hold and remove brads,
pins; may or may not be
equipped with wire-cutter.

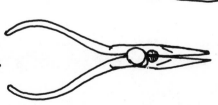

Diagonal side-cut-
ters (ranging from
small model-makers'
tools to 8-inch
long carpenters'
size) are used to
cut off nail and
brad heads and pins
and to cut lengths
of various wires.

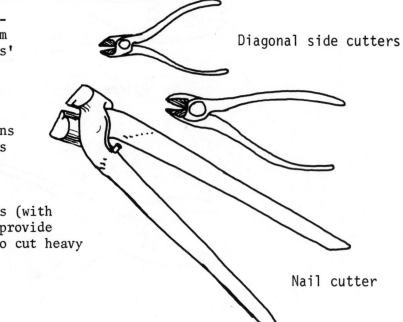

Diagonal side cutters

Large nail cutters (with
10-inch handles) provide
enough leverage to cut heavy
nails and wire.

Nail cutter

Measuring Tools

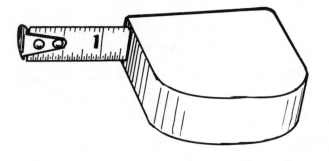

Flexible Steel Tapes are
made in 6-, 8-, 10-, and
12-foot lengths; 1/2-inch
or 3/4-inch wide. For
most use a 10-foot long,
3/4-inch wide tape will be
practical. Buy a tape that
has a locking action. When
the tape is released to return to the case, stop the
action about 2 inches from the end of the tape and feed the
remainder in slowly so as not to rip off the rivets attaching
the little end tab.

A Combination
Square has a
sliding head,
tightened by

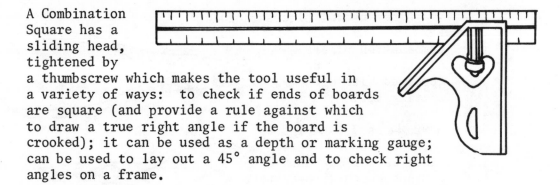

a thumbscrew which makes the tool useful in
a variety of ways: to check if ends of boards
are square (and provide a rule against which
to draw a true right angle if the board is
crooked); it can be used as a depth or marking gauge;
can be used to lay out a 45° angle and to check right
angles on a frame.

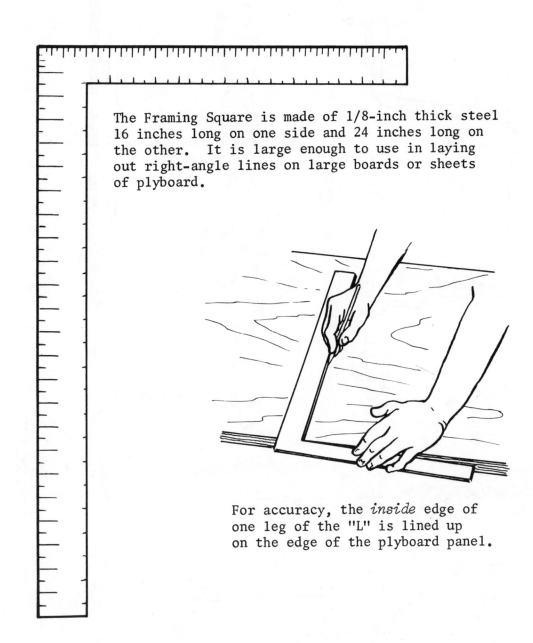

The Framing Square is made of 1/8-inch thick steel 16 inches long on one side and 24 inches long on the other. It is large enough to use in laying out right-angle lines on large boards or sheets of plyboard.

For accuracy, the *inside* edge of one leg of the "L" is lined up on the edge of the plyboard panel.

An Aluminum Carpenter's Level, 24-inches long, provides an accurate check for horizontal place-ment of all cardboard, plastic, or plaster label letters, printed labels, mounting of picture frames, brackets, or picture moldings.

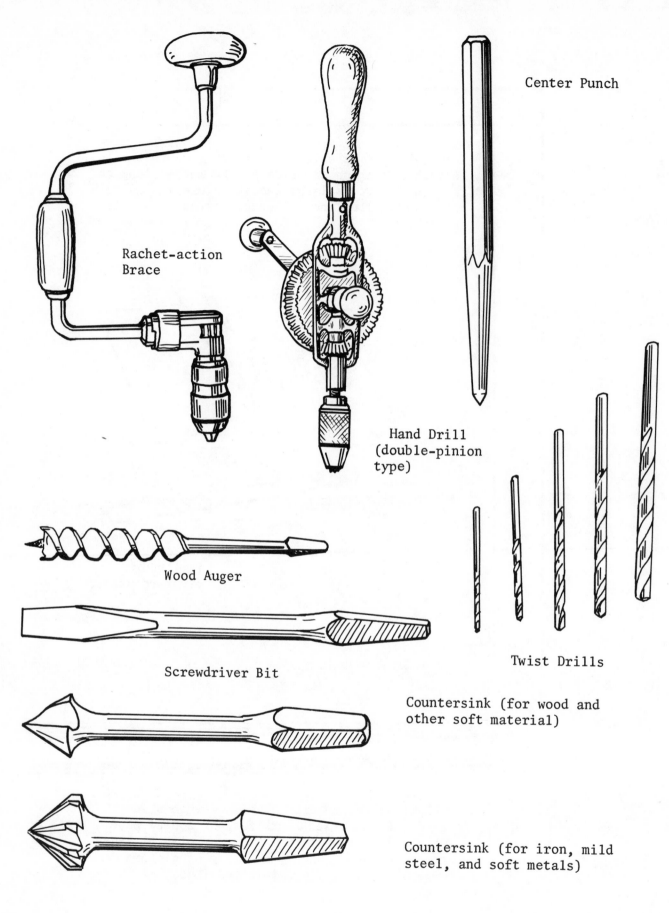

Rachet-action
Brace

Hand Drill
(double-pinion
type)

Center Punch

Wood Auger

Screwdriver Bit

Twist Drills

Countersink (for wood and
other soft material)

Countersink (for iron, mild
steel, and soft metals)

116

Electric drills have nearly replaced the use
of the brace and bit and hand drills, but these are
still useful tools to include in any basic set. The
Hand Drill is used for lightweight work, to drill
holes for screws, nails, etc. The double-pinion
type (with gears on opposite sides of the drive
wheel) is sturdy and long-lasting. The Brace should
be a rachet type to permit heavier work in close
quarters.

A Center Punch should be used to make a starting dent in any material before drilling.

Twist Drills come in sets of eight, from 1/16-
inch to 11/64-inch and are used with both the hand
drill and electric drill. Buying cheap sets is false
economy, for the drills will become dull almost with
first use and may bend or even break with little
pressure.

Wood Augers come in short, medium, and long
lengths as well as in a variety of diameters. Use
the shortest length practical to gain the greatest
control of the tool.

One of the most useful accessories for the
brace is the screwdriver bit. Several sizes may be
purchased. Where a project involves placement of a
quantity of screws, holes for the screws should be
drilled first, the screws well started with a hand
screwdriver, then the brace with screwdriver bit
used to complete driving the screws. Use of the
brace permits fast work and, if a large screw is
difficult to turn by hand, the brace provides greater leverage.

117

Planes most commonly are used to smooth rough places, to bevel edges, and to trim oversize pieces.

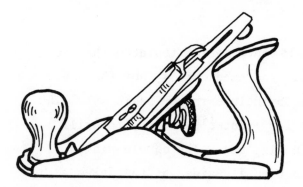

Smoothing plane

While many sizes and styles of planes are made, the Smoothing Plane and Block Plane are most useful for general work.

When using the smoothing plane, be sure to check the grain of the wood and plane *with* the grain and not against it.

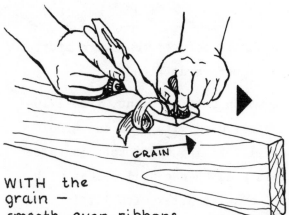

WITH the grain — smooth, even ribbons curl out.

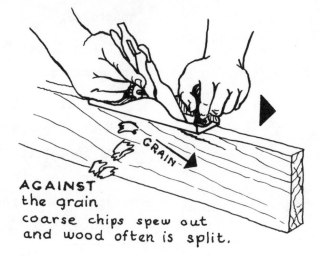

AGAINST the grain coarse chips spew out and wood often is split.

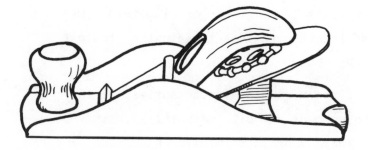

Block plane

The Block Plane, with a blade set at a low angle, is particularly useful for trimming and smoothing end cuts across the grain. Work from the corners to the middle to avoid splitting wood.

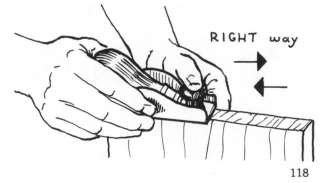

RIGHT way

WRONG!

118

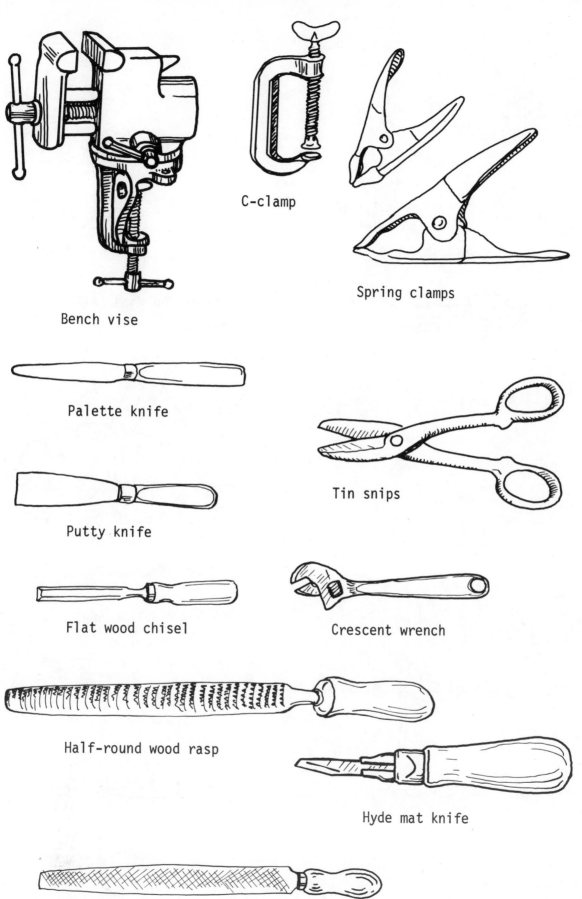

Bench vise

C-clamp

Spring clamps

Palette knife

Putty knife

Tin snips

Flat wood chisel

Crescent wrench

Half-round wood rasp

Hyde mat knife

Mill-bastard cut file

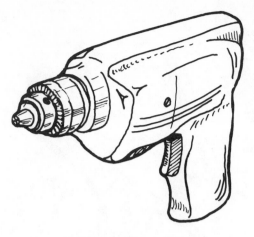

Electric drill

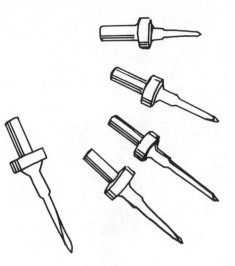

Combination Wood Drill and
Countersinks

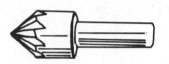

Countersink

Portable electric saw

Saber or jig saw

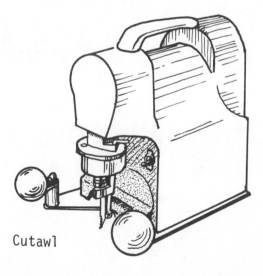

Cutawl

Basic Power Tools

　　　While all construction can be accomplished with
hand tools, power tools increase accuracy and reduce
the time necessary for the same work. Just as with
hand tools, buy the best quality you can and take proper
care of them. Cheap power tools will burn out quickly.
Being made of light weight materials, they will get
out of line and, by failing to deliver accuracy when
it is expected, create frustrations and disappointment.

　　　The Electric Drill is one of the most versatile
tools available and should be the first power tool purchased. Size of the drill indicates the largest diameter of shank that can be held in the chuck. Recently,
3/8-inch drills have taken over some of the popularity
reserved for the earlier 1/4-inch "home handyman" drills.
A 3/8-inch drill with variable speed control, speeds from
0 to 1000 RPM, a motor developing up to 1/3 HP, equipped
with a Jacobs chuck (a geared chuck tightened by a geared
key, *not* a hex-key) will provide a dependable source
of power not only for basic drilling operations, but also
for a variety of attachments.

　　　Bits available for use with the electric drill
range from the 1/16-inch twist drill to a 1-inch spade
bit. Adjustable expansion bits, hole saws with pilot
bits, and combination wood drills and countersinks increase the usefulness of the tool.

　　　With the use of well-made attachments, this
versatile tool can be changed into: a jig or saber
saw, circular saw, sander, grinder, polisher, lathe,
or drill press. A wire brush (bristles come in soft,
medium, or hard) can be used with the drill to clean
rust from metal, or sculpture a textured surface into
plyboard.

The greatest enemy of the drill, as with all power equipment, is dust. Keep the drill in a dust-free cabinet or case, or covered, and follow the manufacturer's directions for proper lubrication and maintenance.

As finances permit, the power Saber (or Jig) Saw and Portable Electric (Circular) Saw should be added to shop equipment.

The Saber Saw makes it possible to cut curved lines in heavy plyboard sheets, window openings in plyboard panels, as well as performing most hacksaw jobs. New heavy-duty models are equipped with variable-speed motors (which develop 1/3 HP), increasing the control and power of the saws. Quarter-inch shank blades range from 2 3/4-inches to 3 1/2-inches in length with from 6 to 10 teeth per inch for wood cutting, to 18 and 32 teeth per inch for metal work.

A 7 1/2-inch (which refers to the diameter of saw blade) industrial-duty Circular Saw with 5/8-inch arbor and 2 HP motor will greatly reduce the time and effort needed in trimming 2x4 and other framing lumber, and cutting full-sized plyboard sheets. Standard combination blades are designed for all types of wood, with and across the grain. Special plyboard blades considerably reduce the amount of splintering when plyboard or thin veneers are cut. Both the combination and plyboard blades should be sharpened and set by a professional. Some companies carry disposable blades which cannot be sharpened or set, but are inexpensive enough to throw away and replace when they become dull. These blades remain sharp and effective for a surprisingly long time.

NEVER RUN A SAW BLADE (Circular *or* Saber) THROUGH

ANY NAILS, SCREWS, OR BOLTS. (It will
ruin the blade and may cause an accident.)

The Cutawl is an amazing cutting tool which
works with a pivoting, reciprocating chisel or blade.
It is used in as widely divergent industries as garment
manufacturing, where it cuts through many thicknesses
of fabric at a time, to department store display and
industrial trade-fair exhibit shops, where it may be
used to cut intricate scroll work (as fine as a jig-
saw puzzle) or sheets of Upson board for theatrical
stage-sets. If your local department stores have their
own display shops, ask if you may see the Cutawl demon-
strated. For information about the tool, write: The
Cutawl Corporation, Bethel, Connecticut 06801.

The following useful power tools may be added
to the basic equipment as funds are available: orbital
sander, jig-saw, radial-arm saw, table saw, and router.

MATERIALS

Most exhibits are built with some combination of framing lumber (for strength) and panel surfacing.

Framing Materials

Pine provides the best framing material. Fir is also used (as in 2x4s), but splits more easily than pine. Use the least expensive grade that will serve the purpose. "Clear" or "Select" is the highest quality and is required *only* when the framing will show and the materials are to be stained rather than painted. The other "finishing" grades are: "C Select" -- next in quality -- may have pin knots and minor imperfections; "D Select" -- lowest in finishing grades -- good for all-round projects. "Board" grades range from No. 1 (with small, solid knots), through No. 5 -- the poorest quality, suitable only for crating.

For most panel and case framing, and general all-round exhibit use, the "D" finishing grade, No. 1 board or No. 2 board grades, are the most practical.

Lumber sizes

The beginning carpenter may feel he is being cheated when he orders and pays for a "1x4" and finds, when he gets it home, that the board actually measures about 3/4-inch thick and 3 5/8-inches wide. It is a common misunderstanding. The finished stock one buys at the lumber yard is referred to in its "nominal" size -- its original, rough-sawed condition. Drying and preparation of the board from rough-sawed to the finished, planed condition yields the final smooth material. The chart opposite shows the "nominal" (rough-sawed size -- the size you order) and the actual size of the finished board.

Lumber yards stock boards in standard lengths,

Lumber sizes

NOMINAL	ACTUAL
1 x 2	3/4 x 1 5/8
2 x 2	1 5/8 x 1 5/8
1 x 3	3/4 x 2 5/8
2 x 3	1 5/8 x 2 5/8
1 x 4	3/4 x 3 5/8
2 x 4	1 5/8 x 3 5/8
1 x 6	3/4 x 5 5/8
1 x 8	3/4 x 7 1/2
1 x 10	3/4 x 9 1/2
1 x 12	3/4 x 11 1/2

usually starting at 8 feet long and increasing by
two-foot lengths. It is usually less expensive,
if you need a 7-foot board, to buy the 8-foot
length and trim it yourself. You would probably
have to pay the 8-foot length anyway, and might
be charged a cutting fee.

DO NOT ASSUME, because you have ordered
8-foot lengths, that all boards will be a *true*
length. Many boards will be at least 1/4-inch
longer. A few (out of a large order) may be
1/8-inch shorter. NEVER ASSUME board ends are
square. Whenever you are building framing for
a panel *always* check the ends with the combination
square.

The best way to buy lumber is to *go to the
yard* and *to check the boards* as the lumberman pulls
them from stock. You have the right to reject any
boards that seem warped (do not buy *any* that are

twisted like a propeller!), have too many knots, or
have loose knots which may work out as the lumber is
used.

Panel Materials

Standard 4-foot by 8-foot sheets of building
materials, unlike board sizes, can be depended upon
(as a rule) to be the full 4x8 size.

AD Interior grade fir plyboard is the most
commonly used material for panels, cases, case furniture,
and lighting fixture enclosures. The 1/4-inch thickness is strong enough for cases displaying small,
lightweight objects; the 3/8-inch thickness is better
for all-round use. Half-inch and 3/4-inch sheets are
used for case bases and platform construction.

Particle board is made from sawdust and chips
mixed with resin and formed into 4 x 8 sheets. It
is less expensive than plyboard, but will not hold
screws as well.

Hardboard (such as Masonite) is also used for
panel construction. It is made in 1/8-inch, 3/16-inch,
and 1/4-inch thicknesses. Both tempered (for exterior
use) and untempered (softer) are available. It is
difficult to pound nails into any hardboard; screws
are more practical to use.

Upson board, made in a wide range of thicknesses
and interior or exterior grades, is one of the most
versatile and least expensive display materials. Most
lumber yards stock sizes 4-feet wide, 6, 8, and 12 feet
long. The 1/8-inch thickness, called "Easy Curve."
permits making background panels with curved surfaces
(which are supported by pine and plyboard framing) and

126

is so flexible it can be made into a 12-inch diameter cylinder. Panels may be made of the 3/16-inch thickness framed with 1 x 2 lumber and suspended in place by being bolted to 2 x 3s wedged between ceiling and floor with spring-loaded caps.

Other sheet materials include Homosote and Cellotex -- both primarily insulating boards; and Fome-Core -- an extremely light weight sheet of expanded plastic (similar to Styrofoam) backed on both sides with Kraft paper (similar to brown wrapping paper). It comes in 3/16-inch, 1/4-inch, and 1/2-inch thicknesses in 4 x 8 sheets. It is cut best with a sharp knife or an extremely fine saw blade. It is an excellent material for large cut-outs.

Corrugated cardboard is also used -- often to achieve a textural effect -- in case backgrounds and to form the sides of curved case furniture (where support is provided by hidden boards). Colors of decorative display corrugated cardboards will fade quickly and should not be considered permanent. The cardboard should be painted for any long-term exhibit.

Adhesives

Liquid white (polyvinyl resin) glue, most often packaged in plastic squeeze bottles, is a good, all-purpose adhesive. It is used in wood joints (both framing and panel-to-frame) and for gluing 3-D letters for labels. The white color turns translucent as the glue dries.

Other white glues are casein-based, excellent for most purposes, but not waterproof and may be affected by humidity and/or high temperature. Check the label to determine if the white glue has a liquid resin or casein base.

Urea resin glue ("Weldwood" is one trade name) comes as a powder. Four parts of the powder are mixed with one part cold water to make a heavy paste. More water is added until the mix is about as thick as heavy cream. It is a good idea to let the mix stand about half an hour before using, but then must be used within four hours. Mix only as needed. Joints must fit tightly.

Epoxy, a two-part glue, will handle most spot-gluing jobs (mineral specimens, dinosaur repairs). It is a *very permanent* kind of glue. Expense limits its use in museum situations.

Beeswax may be melted and mixed with a small amount of turpentine to form a soft, sticky, malleable ball for anchoring stone artifacts and other small objects to sloping panels.

Fasteners

Framing, panels, cases, and case furniture are held together by glue and by nails, screws, or bolts. Joints may be strengthened by the use of metal

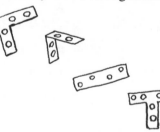 flat corner braces,

angle corner braces,

flat "mending" plates, or

"Tee" braces.

Nails most often used in exhibit construction are box and finishing nails (for framing, panel, case, and case furniture construction) wire nails and brads (for lightweight work -- label fastening, etc.). Box nails

128

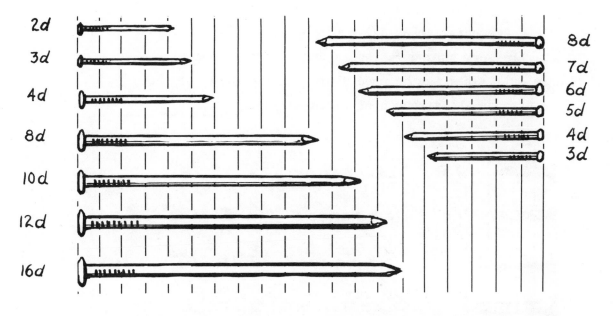

2d	
3d	8d
4d	7d
8d	6d
10d	5d
12d	4d
16d	3d

Actual size drawings: Box and Finishing Nails

are thinner than "common" nails and less apt to split wood. Wire nails (as cigar-box nails) are small nails 1-inch or shorter, with a head; brads are nails 1-inch long or shorter, with no heads (as finishing nails).

Nails are measured by "penny" size. To find the correct "penny" size, measure the length of the nail, subtract 1/2-inch and multiply by 4. Thus, a 2 1/2-inch long nail is an 8 penny nail -- written "8d".

To decide what length of nail to use, choose one about three times as long as the board being nailed.

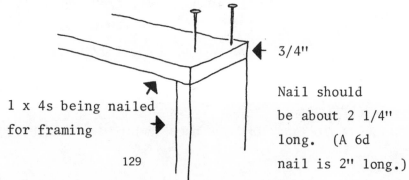

1 x 4s being nailed for framing

3/4"

Nail should be about 2 1/4" long. (A 6d nail is 2" long.)

129

"Cement-coated" nails (dipped in resin or shellac) are very strong fasteners and almost impossible to
draw out. They may be used where framing will not show,
to increase the strength of glued-and-nailed joints.

#5   Size range: ⅜" to ¾"

#6   Size range: ⅜" to 1½"

#7   Size range: ⅜" to 1½"

#8   Size range: ½" to 2"

#10 Size range: ⅝" to 2¼"

#12 Size range: ⅞" to 2½"

Commonly Used Flathead Wood Screws

Screws provide greater holding power than nails
and have the additional advantage of pulling pieces together. They should be used wherever more strength is
required. The list below shows minimum sizes of flathead screws recommended for fastening plyboard sheets
to a supporting frame. Longer screws should be used
when possible.

PLYBOARD	SCREW
1/4 inch	#4, 3/4" long
3/8"	#6, 1"
1/2"	#6, 1 1/4"
5/8"	#8, 1 1/4"
3/4"	#8, 1 1/2"

Bolts and nuts are used in building exhibits which

130

will be taken down and stored. Very handy devices,
often used in furniture manufacture, are "Tee-nuts"
 which can be driven into a pre-
drilled hole in wood to provide
metal threads for bolts. They
are useful particularly where it will be difficult
to hold a regular nut for tightening. The prongs
of the Tee-nut are pulled into the wood as the bolt
is tightened, keeping the nut from turning and pre-
venting it from falling out when the bolt is removed.
Sizes are: 8-32, 10-24, 1/4-20 (most common, and
used with either a 1/4-inch 20 thread stove or
machine bolt), 5/16-18, and 3/8-16.

PANEL CONSTRUCTION: 4' x 8' Panel

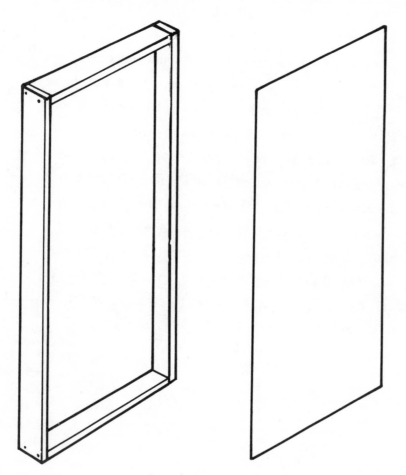

Framing requirements:

   2 1"x4"x8' B grade pine
   2 1"x4"x3'10 1/2" B grade pine

Panel requirement: 1 3/8"x4'x8' AD plyboard

Use white liquid resin glue, 8d coated box nails for
framing; 4d finishing nails to fasten panel to frame.

Procedure:

Glue and nail frame together. Spread glue on frame;
place panel on frame; line up panel with frame along
one eight-foot side. Don't worry if rest of frame is
out of line. Use finishing nails and fasten panel to
frame along the one eight-foot side. After nailing
down one long side, push frame into place on other
sides, lining up with panel. Complete nailing panel
to frame, using finishing nails.

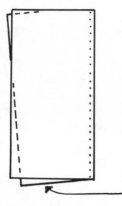

Panel construction: 8' x 8' Panel

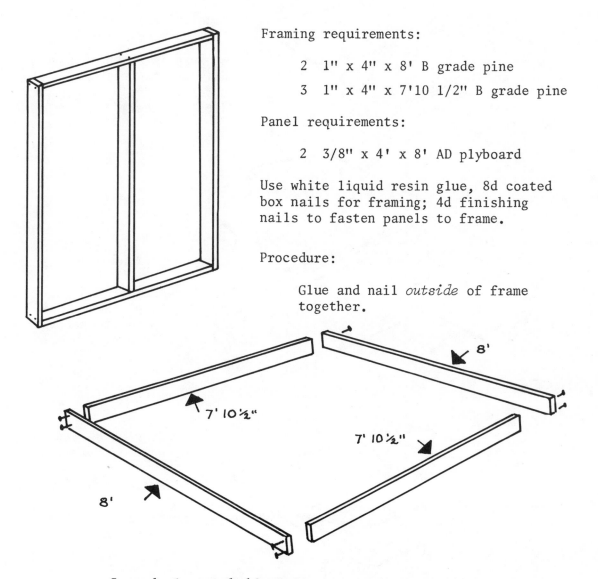

Framing requirements:

   2 1" x 4" x 8' B grade pine

   3 1" x 4" x 7'10 1/2" B grade pine

Panel requirements:

   2 3/8" x 4' x 8' AD plyboard

Use white liquid resin glue, 8d coated
box nails for framing; 4d finishing
nails to fasten panels to frame.

Procedure:

   Glue and nail *outside* of frame
   together.

Spread glue on *half* of frame. Place *one* 4'x8' panel on
   this part of frame.

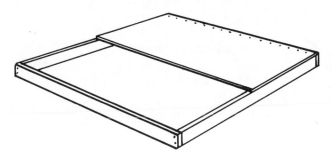

Line up panel on long (8') outside
edge of frame.

Drive in finishing nails on this
long edge, then push frame into
line and nail panel to frame on
top and bottom.

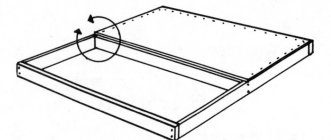

Glue and nail center *framing member* in place.

Be sure it extends only half of its thickness under top panel. (See detail below.)

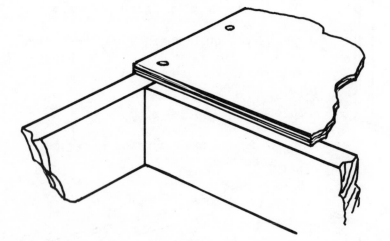

Spread glue on center framing member under top panel. Nail panel to center framing member.

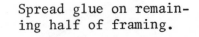

Spread glue on remaining half of framing.

Put second panel in place, butting up against first panel as tightly as possible.

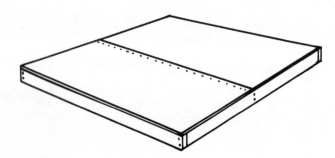

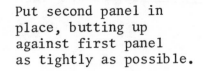

Nail second panel to *center* framing member *first*, then line up rest of frame with panel and finish nailing panel to frame.

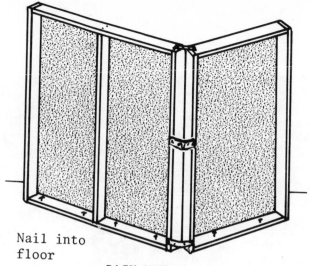

Nail into
floor

BACK VIEW

Placing Frames in Position

6" mending plate screwed to top;

Nails driving through bottom
framing member into floor.

Nails should be driven to within
1/2" of head so they may be removed if a change in wall direction is desired.

Wall must not extend more than
12' in a straight line. Panels
must angle to make wall rigid
and strong.

If panels cannot be nailed to
floor, use mending plates
across back of frames. Mending
plate may be bent to desired
angle by placing in vise, then
bending with pliers.

One end of panel wall should be
fastened to room wall. Use 6"
angle corner brace. Additional
rigidity may be secured by
fastening 1x4 brace from top of
panel framing to room wall.

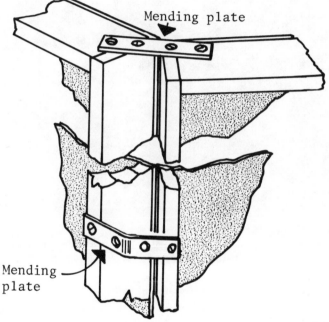

Mending plate

Mending
plate

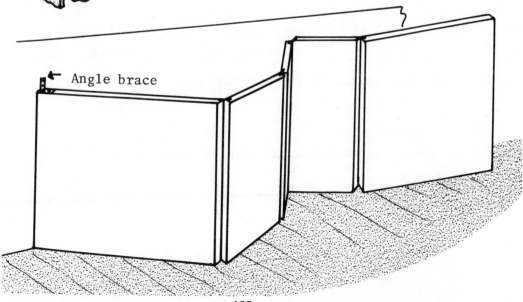

Angle brace

135

Red Men Hall Museum, Empire, Colorado

    As exhibit materials become available and as
funds are obtained for additional building materials,
openings may be cut into panels and cases built behind
them. Until such time, panels may be used to display
photographs, drawings, maps, prints, graphs, etc.
This permits great flexibility in designing a room
installation.

CASE CONSTRUCTION (for panel wall)

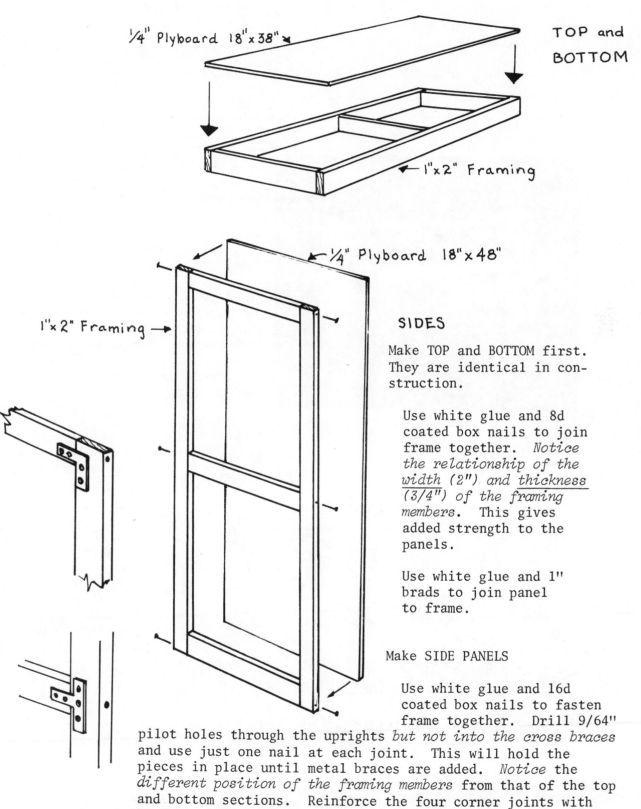

¼" Plyboard 18"x38"

TOP and BOTTOM

1"x2" Framing

¼" Plyboard 18"x48"

1"x2" Framing

SIDES

Make TOP and BOTTOM first. They are identical in construction.

Use white glue and 8d coated box nails to join frame together. *Notice the relationship of the width (2") and thickness (3/4") of the framing members.* This gives added strength to the panels.

Use white glue and 1" brads to join panel to frame.

Make SIDE PANELS

Use white glue and 16d coated box nails to fasten frame together. Drill 9/64" pilot holes through the uprights *but not into the cross braces* and use just one nail at each joint. This will hold the pieces in place until metal braces are added. *Notice* the *different position of the framing members* from that of the top and bottom sections. Reinforce the four corner joints with 3" flat corner braces; reinforce the center piece with two flat 3" "Tee" braces (one at each end) being careful to place the metal braces so the screws will not run into the nails.

Use white glue and 1" brads to join side panels to framing.

ASSEMBLY OF CASE

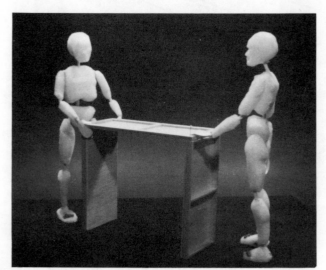

Finish in one day so glue does not set completely until case is put together and square.

Fastening sides to top and bottom:

Have someone help hold pieces in place; TOP and BOTTOM resting on end, with panel surfaces facing; one side piece is fastened to top and bottom with white glue and two 10d coated box nails (1).

Use a countersink drill to make holes for two #10 flathead wood screws 1 1/2" long (2).

Repeat steps for other side.

Lay open frame "box" down on floor with front side down.

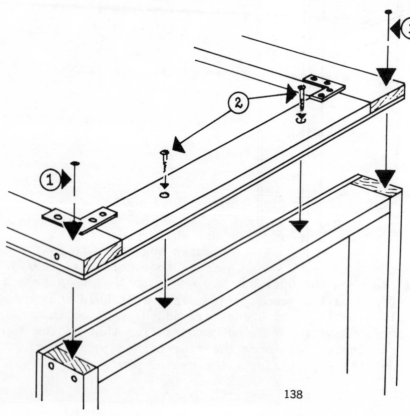

Fasten BACK PANEL to case box with white glue and 3d coated box nails. Be *sure* panel is cut *square* at all corners. Nail panel down along one long edge spacing nails at about 6" intervals, then pull case box into correct alignment and put a nail in the center of each of the other three sides to hold case in line.

Add wired and mounted 3-foot fluorescent fixture to top of case. Use white glue and 10d coated box nails, driving nails through sides into fixture-mounting board which is set in flush with front of case box.

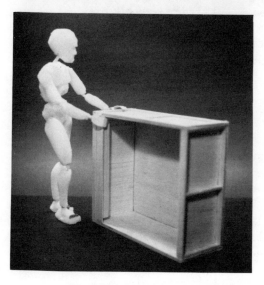

Side leg units are made of 2x2 pine, 31" long, with 13"-long cross-braces and 5"-long vertical cleats (for attachment to case box). These units are fastened together with two 1x2 pine rails about 40" long (check outside measurement of case box). Make all joints with white glue and 6d coated box nails.

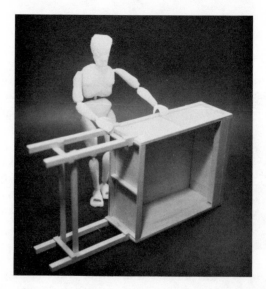

With case box resting on
its side, attach completed
leg units. Line up legs
flush with *back edge* of
case box so that the box
overhangs the front legs
by at least 4". This is
to permit the case front
to be pulled up snug to
panel. Attach legs to
box with white glue and
#8 flathead wood screws
1 1/4" long.

Drill 3/8" hole in bottom center of each leg and
insert stem of 2" caster.

Preparing panel for case exhibit:

Mark off a three-foot square opening, bottom edge to
be 36" from floor. Use carpenter's level to be sure
window opening is level with floor. Use framing
square with level to be sure corners of opening are
square. Drill holes through the panel *from front to
back* (to avoid splitting wood from front surface) in
each corner, using a 3/8" spade bit with the electric
drill. Use a saber saw to cut out the 3'x3' opening.

(1) Reinforce back of panel
with one 1x4 pine board
extending full width,
inside vertical framing
and flush on top edge
with bottom of window
opening.

(2) Reinforce top of window
opening with 1x2 pine
36" long, flush with
top edge of window
opening.

(3) Reinforce sides of window
opening with 1x4 pine
3' 4" long, set in flush
with window opening.

(4) Place 1x4 brace 3' 10 1/2"
long across top of vertical
window braces.

Use white glue and #7 flathead wood screws 3/4" long on all panel braces.

"Shadow box" frame is made of 1x10 pine; top and bottom boards are 35 7/8" long, sides are 34 3/8" long.

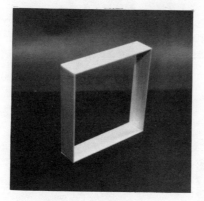

Top and bottom pieces overlap sides.

The pieces are cut 1/8" shorter than window dimensions to make it easier to insert frame in opening.

Use white glue and 8d finishing nails to construct frame.

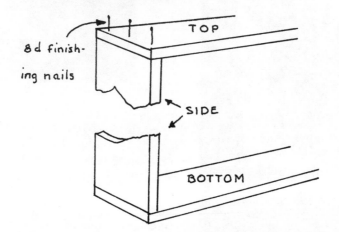

Insert frame in reinforced, rough-cut window opening. Line up back of frame flush with back edge of reinforcing braces.

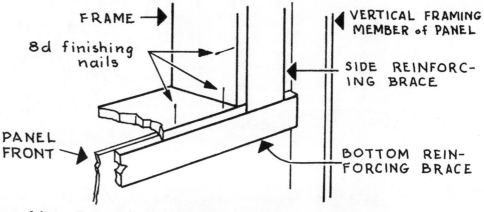

Use white glue and 8d finishing nails to fasten frame in

place driving nails through bottom piece of frame into bottom reinforcing brace. Use framing or combination square to check corners for accuracy before using glue and nails to fasten remaining sides. *Be very careful* to install frame so that corners are *square*. An off-square frame will make glass installation very difficult.

Use 3/4" quarter-round or base shoe molding to trim between shadow-box frame and panel front. Attach with white glue and 1" brads; set nails 1/16" below surface; fill with spackling paste. The molding will hide the rough-cut opening.

Quarter-round back glass stop

7/32" Crystal weight glass

Quarter-round front glass stop

Use 1 1/2" brads to attach strips of quarter-round for glass stops. Install back stops first, bottom strip flush with

back edge of frame.   Side stops hold glass on slant
from top to bottom.

Use 7/32" crystal weight glass. Have it cut 1/4"
shorter than inside dimensions of frame in both
length and width. It will be easier to tip into
place (put bottom edge in first) and the thickness
of the molding strips will hide any gaps.

Fastening case to panel

Roll case into position behind panel. Put heavy-
duty screw-eye in back edge of panel framing (even
with middle brace of side of case).

Put screen-door hook in back vertical brace of
side of case, even with middle brace.

Fasten turnbuckle to screw-eye in panel using a
length of bailing wire.

Screen-door hook is slipped through eye of turnbuckle and case is drawn up tight to panel by
tightening turnbuckle.

It is a good idea to glue a continuous strip of
foam-rubber weatherstripping all around the front
edge of the case (where the case contacts the panel)
to help keep dust from entering the case.

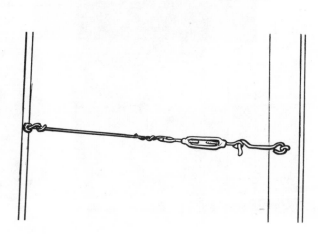

Panel wall and cases   *Red Men Hall Museum, Empire, Colorado*

Diorama opening cut in back of case; associated materials exhibited in case.

"Behind the scenes": Exhibit case behind panel wall; diorama fastened directly to case.

Turnbuckles loosened, screen-door hooks unfastened, and case pulled away from panel. *(More recent design installs light directly in case.)*

Wiring and Installing a Fluorescent Light Fixture

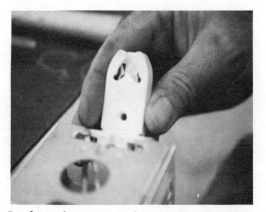

Disassembled fixture (as shipped)

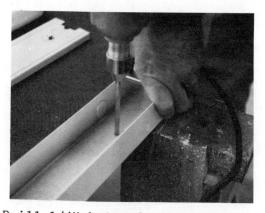

Drill 1/4" holes for mounting bolts (if needed).

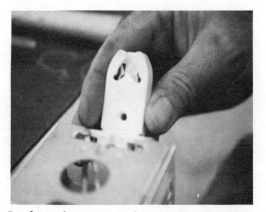

Socket is snapped in place and

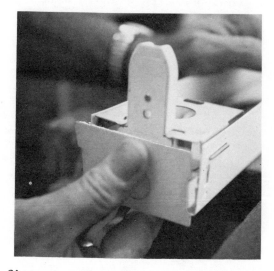

fixture end pushed in place.

After deciding from which end cord is to run, remove knock-out plug.

Install Romex connector
in hole. (This protects
cord from chafing against
metal edge and helps to
keep wire from pulling
out.)

Use 14 gauge SJO 3-wire
(grounded) cord. The three
wires will be colored black,
white, and green.

In the fixture there may be
several colors of wires.
Use *only* the black and white
being *sure* to join the black
wire of the cord to the black
wire of the fixture, and the
same with the white.

Ballasts in some fixtures are
equipped with a short wire,
about 3/4" long, on one end
to which the green (ground)
wire may be attached, using
a plastic wire connector
(wire nut).

If the ballast does not have
a grounding wire, the green
wire of the cord may be attached to the mounting bolts
which hold the ballast in
place.

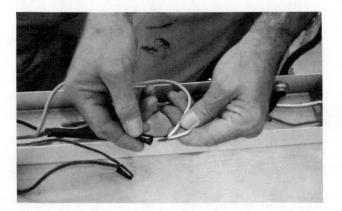

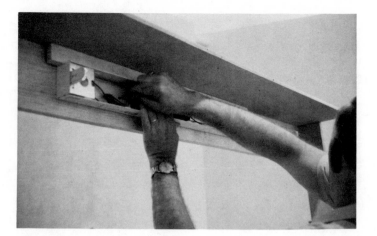

Use fixture for guide when marking
location of bolt holes to be drilled through mounting board. Use a
1 1/2"-wide scrap board as a spacer
to be sure top of fixture will be
down 1 1/2" from top of case.

Drill holes through mounting board
and countersink on front side of
wood (to permit flush fit of 3"-
long 1/4" flathead bolts which are
used to fasten fixture to board.

Push bolts through mounting board
from front side. If working alone,
hold bolts in place with strips of
masking tape.

Hang 1/2"x1 1/2" pipe
nipples over bolts on
inside of case to serve
as spacers to hold fix-
ture a safe distance
from board (overheated
ballasts may sometimes
cause fires).

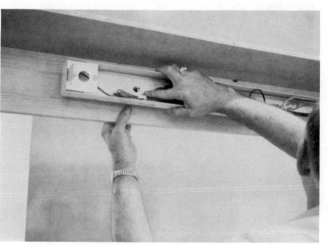

Hang fixture on bolts,
add nuts and tighten.

Drill 7/8" hole through end of
wood case through which cord
will run and insert 1/2"x1 1/2"
pipe nipple attaching with
threaded plastic grommets on
each end. This protects the
cord from rough edges of wood.
Pull free end of cord from
fixture through pipe nipple to
outside of case.

Use rubber 3-wire cap for
grounding type receptacles.

The plug will have three
screws: brass, silver, and
a hexagonal green screw.

Be sure to attach the green
wire of the cord to the
green screw of the plug;
the black wire to the brass
screw, and the white wire to
the silver.

Two single-tube, 3-foot fluorescent
lights mounted in a 7-foot case.

CASE HISTORY of a Case

Four pieces of 1/2" thick plyboard temporarily are tacked
together with 4d nails.

A pattern curve made from a
folded length of wrapping
paper (folded to make a sym-
metrical curve) is traced
on the boards.

The boards are cut with
electric saber saw.

Two pieces of curve are
used for ends; two are
fastened together with
glue and 4d coated box
nails (clinched over on
ends) to form a 1"-thick
center section.

These sections are joined
by 1x4s attached with glue
and 4d coated box nails.

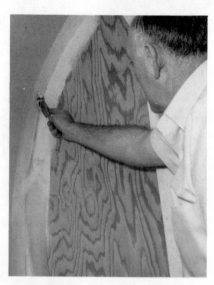

"Easy-Curve" Upson Board is fitted to frame and trimmed, but not fastened.

Frame is installed in case then Upson board is added.

Joints are sealed with tape and paste.

All pieces are checked for fit

before final painting and modeling are done.

THE ICE AGE WORLD OF ANCIENT MAN

150

Construction of case
furniture with curved
sides

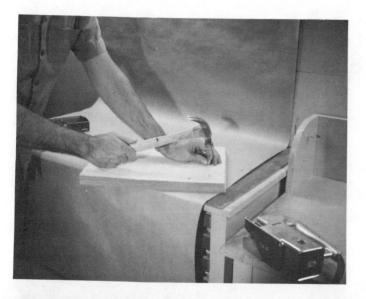

Two pieces of Cellotex temporarily
are joined together with nails.
Nails are put through scrap area
of pieces.

Bottom left: Saber saw is used to
cut through both pieces at once
along the curve.

Bottom right: White glue and 3d
finishing nails are used to fasten
the bottom piece of Cellotex to
lengths of scrap lumber.

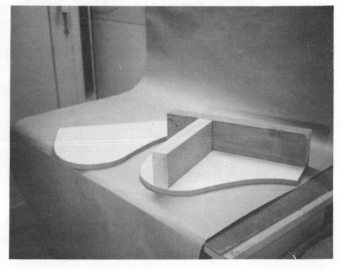

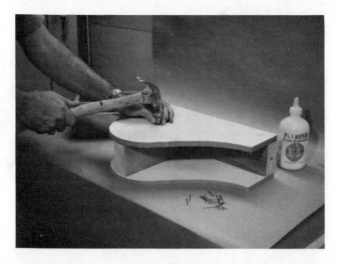

White glue and 3d finishing
nails are used to fasten top
piece of Cellotex in place.
Nails are set just below surface and holes filled with
spackling paste.

White glue and straight pins
hold a strip of corrugated
cardboard in place. Cardboard may be applied with
corrugations exposed (as here)
or with smooth side out.
Weight of displayed object is
supported by interior pieces
of wood.

When glue has set, pins are
removed and cardboard is
trimmed with sharp X-Acto
knife.

Cardboard should be painted.
Colors of decorative corrugated cardboard will fade.

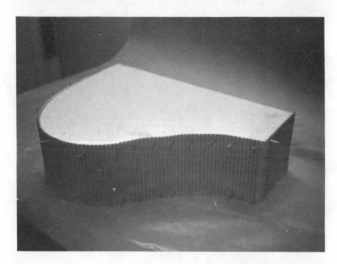

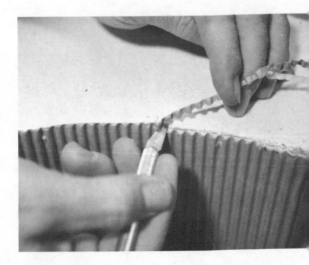

LABELS: Quantity Production of Plaster Letters

(Originally published by the American Association for State and Local History, Technical Leaflet 23)

Three-dimensional letters usually are used for the "headline" and "subhead" labels in a case. While commercially made letters are available it is relatively inexpensive to make 3-D letters. Latex molds are made over a pattern alphabet and as many letters as are needed are then cast with plaster.

Pattern alphabets may be found in lettering books and traced onto tracing paper or onion skin paper with a soft pencil. *Do not use carbon paper and deface the book!* To enlarge letters to a desired size follow the steps outlined below.

a. Original letter
b. Graph of squares drawn over original
c. Graph of same number of squares drawn to desired size.
d. Corresponding points (such as no. 1 and no. 2) are established and the enlarged letter sketched in.

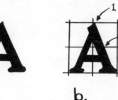

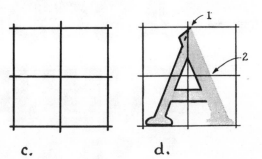

A more accurate way is to ask a photographer friend to make a slide of the alphabet, then project it to the size needed. The alphabets chosen should not be smaller than 3/4" and should not have any parts that are extremely thin, as the final plaster letters probably will break.

Three alphabets are shown on the following pages.

ABCD
EFGH
IJKLM
NOPQ
RSTUV
WXYZ

abcdef
ghijklm
nopqrst
uvwxyz
123456
7890?!;

Roman upper and lower case and numerals.
Good for Colonial Period and Revolutionary War times.

ABCDE
FGHIJK
LM NO
PQRST
UVWX
YZ;!?

Gothic upper case.

abcdef
ghijkl7
mnopq
rstuvw
xyz123
45680

Gothic lower case and numerals.

Trace the pattern alpha-
bet onto masonite or
other hardboard material
at least 1/4" thick.
Drill holes through the
enclosed parts of the
letters A, B, D, O, P,
Q, and R. These holes
should be large enough
for the coping saw blade.

Below left: Letters
drawn on 1/4" masonite,
holes drilled. Scrap
piece of wood with "V"
cut is clamped to table
and provides support for
three sides of letter as
it is cut. A power jig-
saw makes the work easier.

Upper and lower case of the Barnum family.
Good for use in Civil War displays.

Right: Run saw blade through a hole, fasten the blade in the
saw and cut out the enclosed portion. It will be easier

to cut out this part *before* cutting out the entire letter. Unfasten the blade from the saw and remove it from the hole. Replace blade in saw, then complete cutting out the letter.

Sand the letters smooth, rounding the edges. To fill the pores of the material, the letters are given a brush coat of shellac or a spray coat of clear lacquer from a pressure spray can. When they are completely dry they are sanded once more with very fine sandpaper. A light coat of paste floor wax is applied, permitted to dry, and polished with a soft cloth. The final patterns should be *very* smooth. They are placed on one large or several small pieces of scrap plate glass, as an extremely smooth base surface is needed. Sharp edges of scrap glass may be rounded with sandpaper. Wear protective goggles when sanding glass.

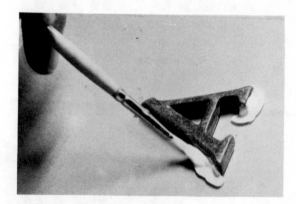

A small paint brush is used with the latex. Wet the brush in water, then work up a lather with a mild soap (such as Ivory hand soap). Gently squeeze the excess lather from the brush, then dip into the latex and anchor the letters by flowing the latex around the edges of the letters where they rest on the glass.

As soon as the letters are anchored, give them a full brush coat of latex. *Watch out for bubbles!* Pop them by blowing on them or by pricking with a pin. Then be sure to wash the brush between each coat of latex. The pre-lathering will

help in getting the brush clean. If something goes
amiss, the dried latex may be removed from the brush
by soaking the bristles in gasoline.

Let each coat of latex dry completely before
adding the next. The color will change from milky
white to a transluscent yellow as the rubber dries.
Apply about eight coats to the letters. Do not try
to fill up the enclosed holes of A, B, D, O, P, Q,
and R, or the rubber will become so stiff that the
plaster letters will be hard to remove without breaking.

After several coats of latex have been applied,
a plaster-of-Paris supporting mold is made. Enclose the
latex-covered letter with strips of wood (which have been
waxed). Note that the placement permits using strips of
random lengths. The strips are held in place with lumps
of oil-base modelling clay and the inside corners of the
"well" are also sealed with clay. Be sure the whole set-
up of glass, "well", and letter is on a level surface.
If the finished supporting mold does not hold the latex
mold level, the cast plaster letter will be thick on one
side and thin on the opposite, resembling a cake baked in
a tilting oven.

157

Measure enough water to fill the "well" at least half way and pour into a plastic or enamelware mixing bowl. (Do not wash out the pans when the plaster has been used. Let the excess plaster dry, then run the pan full of cold water. The plaster will loosen from the enamelware pan or plastic bowl and may be lifted out in a piece.) Sift or shake plaster-of-Paris into the water until an "island" forms. Let the mound of plaster get completely wet, then sift a small additional amount into the water until it begins to form a second mound. Let this plaster absorb the water, stir *gently* to avoid creating air bubbles, then pour into the well. Vibrate the plaster by banging on the table top or by shaking the supporting glass surface. This will drive out trapped air. Let the plaster harden at least two hours. Let the excess plaster harden in the mixing bowl -- to indicate when the mold is sufficiently hard.

When the plaster has set, remove the wooden strips, then take the supporting mold from the latex. The inner plaster surface will be powdery. Peel the rubber mold away from the pattern letter. Dust the inner surface with talc to keep the sides from sticking together.

Give the plaster supporting mold three or four coats of shellac or spray with clear lacquer to seal the surface, then apply a light coat of paste wax. This is to prevent the plaster used in casting the letters from building up and distorting the latex mold.

Place the latex mold in the supporting plaster mold and brush with a 25% solution of hydrochloric (muriatic) acid. Drain the mold. The acid will counteract the ammonia in the latex and will keep the cast plaster letters from being powdery. Apply this acid solution each time you cast a letter for at least the first ten letters. After enough casts have been made, the acid is no longer necessary.

Mix more plaster and spoon into the molds. Try
not to pour in so much plaster that the molds run over.
Vibrate to get out trapped air. Let the plaster set at
least two hours, then remove the letters and trim, if
necessary. They will be easier to trim when they are
first removed from the mold.

After several letters of the same character have
been cast and trimmed, they may be attached to a glass
surface and "gang" molds made so that it is possible to
make several casts of one letter at one time.

Use empty shoe boxes to set up a stock pile of
letters.

Painting and Installing 3-D Letters

"Home-made" plaster letters and commercially
available plaster, plastic, and cardboard letters can
be sprayed easily with a spray gun, air brush, "Flit"
gun, or with spray cans of paint. The letters are
pressed to drafting tape which is mounted on scrap
board with the sticky side up. This process makes it
possible to paint the letters without the necessity of

159

Drafting tape – sticky side up

Sticky side down

holding them in the hand. It also provides a quick
indication of the space the label will occupy.

To put up a label of three-dimensional letters,
tape a yardstick to the background as a guide. (Be
sure the yardstick is not warped.) Use a carpenter's
level to be sure the stick is straight. When starting
a new line, leave at least the height of the letters
as a space between lines; in other words, for 1/2-inch
letters, leave at least a 1/2-inch space between the
bottom of the top line and the *top* of the next line.
Actually, a proportion of one and a quarter of the
letter height is better, or a space of 5/8-inch for
1/2-inch letters. Lines should be *not longer* than
fifty to sixty characters.

Apply a thin "thread" of white glue to the
back of the 3-D letters and press them against the
label surface, using the taped-up yardstick for
a horizontal guide.

LABELS: Other than three-dimensional

(Portions of this section originally were published by the American Association for State and Local History, Leaflet 22)

"Group" and specimen labels may be typeset, but the cost usually is prohibitive. If it is possible to purchase a used display-sign press from a local department store, slowly build up a stock of type, read the Boy Scout Merit Badge booklet on printing, and persuade the town printer to donate consultant advice to the museum (circumstances that have occurred in at least one museum) it might be practical to produce typeset labels. Less effort is involved in typing the labels with a machine equipped with bulletin-sized type, or in mastering hand lettering. If purchase of a "label" typewriter is considered, be sure to choose one which is provided with both upper and lower case letters. Labels which are typed only in caps quickly become difficult for the eye to read. The Royal typewriter company can supply a typewriter provided with 24-point size Bulletin type which is excellent for most purposes. Check also to learn if an oversize carriage is available.

The specimen labels should be printed, typed, or lettered on paper of the same color as the background of the case. Labels that are on cards of a different color simply create twice as many objects in the case competing for attention. It is easy to match paper to the case.

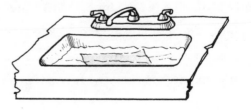

Soak ordinary wrapping paper (Kraft, not slick or coated paper) for about five minutes in warm water. Remove

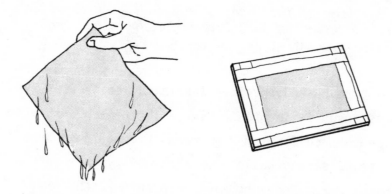

and drain the paper, turning each edge up until it has
drained from all four corners. Place it on plyboard or
an old drawing board and use a squeezed-out sponge to
dampen the wood around the edge of the paper. Tape
down all four edges with gummed paper tape. Lap the
tape about three-quarters of an inch over the edge of
the paper. The paper will be quite wrinkled, but as
it dries it will pull tight and smooth. When the case
and case furniture are painted, this paper should also
be painted. Use a latex or some other matte-finish
paint that is waterproof when dry. The paper again
will wrinkle, but when it has dried it will be tight
and smooth once more. Cut it from the board and print,
type, or letter the label onto it. When the ink is dry,
trim the labels and glue or dry-mount them in place. To
glue them, soak the printed and trimmed labels for a
moment in lukewarm water, then blot between lint-free
towels. Put the label face down and brush the back with
slightly thinned white liquid glue brushing from the
center out to all edges. Put the label in place (on
Easy-Curve, poster board, Masonite, etc.), cover it
with a sheet of waxed paper, and use a linoleum brayer
or any other rubber roller to press the label to the
support and force out trapped air bubbles. With a
slightly dampened sponge, wipe off surplus glue. Put
fresh waxed paper over the surface, cover the label with

162

a flat, texture-free panel (such as Masonite), and
weight it down. Let dry overnight. It is a good
idea to mount a sheet of wrapping paper on the back
side of the label (following the steps just given)
to counteract the pull of the label-paper as it
dries. When both sides have been covered, the label
should be flat and smooth and ready to install in
the case. Dry-mounting may be accomplished with a
pressing iron turned to "low" (linen) and by using
dry-mounting tissue available from photography
stores. A low-melting point, wax-based tissue is
easiest to use. A third method of mounting the
printed label to a support is to use a sheet of
double-coated pressure-sensitive adhesive. This is
a thin sheet of paper which is sticky on both sides.
Covered with a protective sheet on each side, the
sheet may be trimmed to approximate size, one side
of the protective layer removed and the label pressed
down to the adhesive. Final trimming of both the label
and the adhesive sheet to which it is attached may then
be done. The label is put in place by removing the
protective sheet from the back of the adhesive and
pressing the label to the surface. Each placement
must be accurate, there will be no way of lifting,
sliding, or adjusting the label. The advantage of using
this material over the other two methods described is
that the adhesive permanently mounts labels to glass
and metal.

Lettering for Labels

"Instant" lettering, a fairly recent development
in art materials, can be used to produce professional
appearing labels. Called a "dry transfer" method, letters
are printed on translucent plastic sheets. The sheet is

placed on the label paper and the desired letter is rubbed gently. The letter transfers from the plastic to the label paper. Many sizes and styles of letters are available. Check the "Alphabet" listing in the Appendix.

Stencils often may be found in local ten-cent, stationery, and drug stores. These are simple to use and effective in appearance if the letters are completed by filling in. Some styles and sizes are shown on the opposite page.

Gummed paper letters, from 1/4-inch to much larger, are inexpensive and easy to use. To apply, a straight-edge is taped or a line drawn on the label paper and tweezers are used to touch each letter to a slightly dampened sponge and then to put in place.

Large letters: plaster cast in latex molds;

small letters, gummed paper

Close-up of gummed paper letters

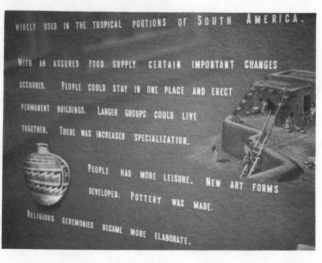

1 inch ROMAN CAPS: letter segments connected and filled in

LETTER

STENCILS

3/4 inch GOTHIC
CAPS

letter outlines traced
guide line and spacing marks above

are available

3/4 inch GOTHIC LOWER CASE: letter segments outlined and
filled in; connecting lines drawn;
guide line and spacing marks above

IN MANY

SIZES AND

STYLES

1/2 inch ROMAN CAPS

Specimens in some exhibits have labels made with a plastic "tape-writer" which presses letters into an adhesive plastic strip. This method is acceptable for a limited quantity of labels.

Hand Lettering

Extensive lettering can be done with lettering guides (LeRoy, Wrico, Rapidesign, Rapidoguide), or by free-hand lettering. Hand-lettered labels may be prepared with the aid of these tools and materials:

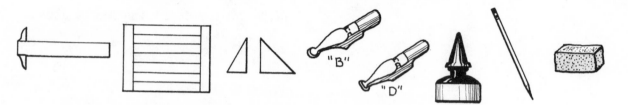

T-square; drawing board; triangles; style "B" and "D" Speedball pen points in penholders; black *waterproof* drawing ink; an ordinary No. 2 lead pencil; art gum eraser, and paper that matches the color of the case.

Do not trim the colored paper to final size until the lettering is complete. It will be easier to fit letters on a size allowing for variation rather than to work on the final size. Try to handle the sheet by the edges and, as you work, protect the surface with a clean piece of paper under both hands. If grease from the natural oils in your hands gets on the surface of the paper it will be difficult for the ink to flow on smoothly.

Tape the colored paper on your drawing board with drafting or masking tape. Use the T-square and a triangle to lay out a series of guide lines, drawing the lines with very light strokes of your pencil. With very light marks, lay out the lettering of the label to check the spacing,

then use the desired pen point, holder, and black ink
to letter the label. Finally, when the ink is thoroughly dry, erase the pencil marks with the art gum eraser.

As with the 3-D letters, try to leave at least
the height of the letters as a space between lines.

The guide lines will be easier to draw if you
drill a series of holes in one of the triangles to use
as guide holes. Use a 1/16-inch drill bit, then use
a larger bit part way through the plastic to make a
tapered hole.

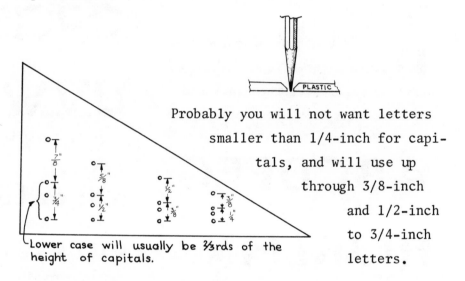

Lower case will usually be ⅔rds of the
height of capitals.

Probably you will not want letters
smaller than 1/4-inch for capitals, and will use up
through 3/8-inch
and 1/2-inch
to 3/4-inch
letters.

Use three-dimensional letters for any letters 3/4-inch
and larger in size.

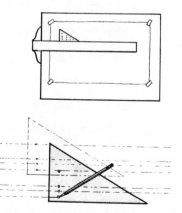

Use the T-square to guide the
triangle across the paper. Draw
the first series of lines, then
line up the top hole with the
bottom line and draw three
more lines. Continue on down
the page.

Drawing the Letters

   You will be able to make all
letters, both capitals (A) and lower
case (a) with combinations of the
six basic strokes shown to the right.

   Two typical alphabets are
shown here. The one to the right
is made with the style "B" round-
tip, Speedball pen point.

   The alphabet below is made
with the style "D" oval-tip Speedball pen point.

   Make a series of guide lines
on a clean paper. Tape a sheet of
tracing paper over the lines and
practice the alphabets until it is

I-\/( )

ABCDEFG
HIJKLMN
OPQRST
UVWXYZ
(UPPER CASE)

abcdefghijklmno
pqrstuvwxyz
(lower case)

possible to draw every
letter from memory.

The C, G, O, and Q will
be easier to draw and
will look better if they
are drawn as wide ovals
rather than true circles.

An excellent and inexpen-
sive booklet, prepared by
the makers of Speedball

ABCDEFG
HIJKLMN
OPQRST
UVWXYZ
(UPPER CASE)

abcdefghijklmno
pqrstuvwxyz
(lower case)

168

pen points, may be obtained from most art supply, office supply, or stationer's stores. The key to even, uniform, and effective hand lettering is *practice!*

Points to Notice

The letters do not all fit into the same width. Compressing a wide letter, such as an M or W to fit into the same width as a narrow letter such as J or S will make the wide letter appear darker, or "heavier" than the rest of the letters in the word. Stretching a narrow letter to fit the space of a wide letter will make it appear "skinny" or "lighter" than the rest of the word.

Only these letters just touch both the top and bottom guide lines: B, D, E, F, H, I, K, L, M, N, P, R, T, X, Y, Z.

Because of an optical illusion the remaining letters are drawn as noted, to make them *appear* to be the same height as the other letters.

The point of the letter A extends just a little above the top line, while the legs rest on the bottom.

The top of the letters J, U, V, and W touch the top guide line, but extend just a little below the bottom line.

The round letters C, G, O, Q, and S extend a little beyond both the top and bottom lines.

The middle bars or lines of a letter vary in height. If all were placed on the true center some would appear high and others low. The letters A, G, P, and R have bars just a little *below* center; B, E,

F, and H have bars a little *above* center.

On some letters it is a good idea to have the upper part a little smaller than the lower, to keep them from appearing top heavy. These are: B, G, K, R, S, X, Z.

One of the most frequent mistakes made by amateurs

PROMINENT FAMILIES
OF MIDDLETOWN

in lettering labels or signs is the mixing of capitals and lower case letters within a single word. Another is to make the slant of the N in the wrong direction; a third is the reversal of the S.

Spacing Between Letters

Because letters carry different *optical* weights, they will not appear properly spaced if they are placed on a line

LOCAL HISTORY
LOCAL HISTORY

so that each letter occupies exactly the same area, or with exactly the same distance between each letter within the word. If a measuring unit is established which is half again as wide as the letter "I" is thick, it can be used to show the correct *proportional* spacing between letters to achieve the correct visual balance.

Use half of this space when the letters A, L, T, V, W, and Y are followed by a straight vertical.

AN, LETTER,
VIE, WIN, YEA

Wedge-shaped letters occurring together, such as A, V, and W, should be kept a full space apart *on the diagonal*.

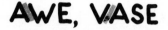

When the round letters C, D, G, O, Q, and S come next to a straight vertical or occur together,  they are placed closer together than the space between two straight vertical letters.

When the letter A is preceded or followed by T or Y, the bottom of the A comes directly under the top of the T or Y. When A follows P the bottom of the A comes directly under the curved part of the P.

When the letter L is followed by T, V, W, or Y the lower right hand corner of the L is directly under the top edge of the other letter.

BELT, ELVES

ALWAYS

A letter which follows "open" letters such as C, E, F, G, K, and P, is placed closer to the open letters than to a straight vertical.

CIDER, FIG, KEG

Spacing Between Words

Use the letters M or W as a measuring unit between words.

171

FINISHING METHODS

Note: All nail holes, cracks, and spaces should be filled with spackling paste; rough places should be sanded smooth. All sanding should be done *with* the grain, not across it.

Upson Board, Cellotex, or plyboard may be painted, covered with textures, or be covered with fabric. Plyboard may also be stained.

Paint:

In general, flat or matte finish, water-thinned paints such as household latex or vinyl interior paints are used for all case exhibit purposes. Usually two coats are required.

Satin-finish oil-base enamels are used on walls and stands that are exposed to public touch. Two coats are applied over a primer-sealer coat.

Painting plyboard:

The grain of plyboard will show through as a definite pattern unless a primer-sealer is used before other finishes are applied. Paint stores can recommend specific products. One of the best is white-pigmented "Firzite" which may be put on with a brush or roller. The plyboard is sanded lightly with very fine (6/0) garnet paper when the Firzite has dried, then it is painted with final coats of latex or vinyl paint.

Staining plyboard:

Ready-mixed stains are made in many colors. Oil stains are easy to use. They should be applied before the wood is sealed. Use a 2-inch or 3-inch flat brush, spreading the stain with the grain. After 10 or 15 minutes wipe off the excess with a rag. A second coat may be applied if a deeper color is desired. Let the wood dry overnight, then

172

seal with a coat of shellac. When the shellac has dried, rub lightly with fine steel wool to dull the gloss.

For an "antique" stain use an oil-based white-pigmented undercoat thinned with turpentine and brush over the surface. Wipe off with a dry cloth after about 10 to 15 minutes. When dry, sand lightly with fine sand-paper. Seal with thinned white shellac (mix about half-and-half with denatured alcohol). Sand again when dry. Use a thinned flat enamel or tinted undercoat in what-ever color desired to wipe on a second color. Let wood dry completely, then seal with one coat of a satin-finish varnish.

Adding Textures to Exhibit Surfaces

Texture paint, which comes as a powder and is mixed with water, may be purchased and applied with a variety of rollers to get differing finishes.

A flock (velvet-like) texture is obtained by spraying the flock particles over a wet, freshly painted surface. Flat-finish enamel is used for a base color-and-adhesive coat. Most vacuum cleaners have flock-guns available as an accessory. At Christmas time many "Sno-Flock" kits include a vacuum-cleaner powered flock gun. Different colors of flock are available from craft supply houses.

A base color-adhesive coat of flat enamel is also used if a layer of sand, gravel, ground cork, used coffee grounds, sawdust, or other texture is desired. These tex-tures may be left their natural colors or spray-painted.

Fabrics may be stretched over a panel and stapled to the back. The material should be folded at least once along the stapled edges. A light spray-mist of water will shrink the cloth enough to pull it smooth.

Cloth may be more permanently attached by applying latex paint over the stretched fabric surface. Use a roller and work the paint well into and through the cloth. The material may sag and wrinkle while it is wet, but usually will tighten as it dries.

A loose-woven fabric such as decorative burlap or monk's cloth may be stretched over a panel of peg-board so that the pattern of peg-board holes is not apparent but the useful qualities of the board are not lost.

APPENDICES

Record Keeping

Suppliers and Manufacturers

Useful Publications

Associations

Record Keeping

A record should be made of each exhibit. This may be kept on file cards or in a looseleaf notebook. The following information should be included in each exhibit's record:

1. Date exhibit completed;

2. Colors used: name of manufacturer, color name *and* formula. (It is a good idea to paint a brush-width swatch of each color next to each color notation.)

3. Manufacturer's names and addresses, and model numbers of any "special-effects" used (automatic slide projectors, turntables, light color filters, etc.);

4. Name of manufacturer and specific kind of light (*very* important for fluorescent lights);

5. List of catalogue numbers of each specimen in the exhibit;

6. A full copy of labels in the case together with main bibliographic references;

7. List of references for any drawn or painted illustrations;

8. List of negative numbers of any photographs used.

Suppliers and Manufacturers

ACETATE SLEEVES (Transparent plastic enclosures --
        often used to protect pages in loose-
        leaf notebooks)

Albany Novelty Mfg.
107 W. Canton St.
Boston, Mass.

Central Plastics
527 So. Wells St.
Chicago, Illinois 60607

C-Line Products, Inc.
1530 E. Birchwood Ave.
Des Plaines, Illinois 60018

Kingsbacher Murphy
9830 Bellama Ave.
Los Angeles, California 90045

Samsill Bros. Plastic
4301 Mansfield Hwy.
Ft. Worth, Texas 76119

Sigo Mfg.
209 W. 26 St.
New York, N.Y. 10001

Transilwrap Co.
4427 N. Clark
Chicago, Illinois 60640

ADHESIVES

Adhesive Products
1660 Boone Ave.
Bronx, N.Y. 10460

Ambroid Co.
305 Franklin St.
Boston, Mass. 02110

Borden Chemical Co.
350 Madison Ave.
New York, N.Y. 10017

Fasson Products ("double-stick" pressure-sensitive sheets)
250 Chester St.
Painesville, Ohio 44077

Adhesives (cont.)

Goodyear Tire and Rubber Co. (Pliobond)
Akron 16, Ohio

Imperial Adhesives, Inc.
6315 Wiehe Rd.
Cincinnati, Ohio 45237

Industrial Adhesive Co.
2500 Caroline St.
Dallas, Texas 75201

Charles Mayer Studios (Hook N'Loop)
Dept. AG-68
776 Commins St.
Akron, Ohio 44307

Slomons, Dept. A67 (Sobo Plastic Resin glue)
L.I. City, New York 11101

3M Co.
2501 Hudson Rd.
St. Paul, Minn. 55119

U.S. Plywood (Weldwood)
777 Third Ave.
New York, N.Y. 10017

Wilhold Glues
8707 Millergrove Dr.
Santa Fe Springs, California 90670

ALPHABETS (3-D)

American Display Associates
Fort Marshall
Sullivan's Island, So. Carolina

Austen Displays, Inc.
133 W. 19th St.
New York, N.Y. 10011

Dicar Letter Co.
231 E. 14th St.
New York, N.Y. 10003

Electra Display and Sales Co.
275 Fifth Ave.
New York, N.Y. 10016

Alphabets (cont.)

Florida Plastics, Inc.
904 4th St.
Palmetto 61, Florida

Grace Letter Co.
77 Fifth Ave.
New York, N.Y.

Kore-Foam Displays, Inc.
1520 E. Adams Blvd.
Los Angeles, California 90011

Mitten's Display Letters
39 W. 60th St.
New York, N.Y. 10023

Redikut Letter Co.
185 No. Prairie Ave.
Hawthorne, Calif.

Scott Plastics Co.
Box 2840
Sarasota, Florida

ALPHABETS ("Flat")

ACS Tape Co. (Instant Lettering)
217 California St.
Newton, Mass. 02158

Artype, Inc.
Crystal Lake, Illinois 60014

Cello-Tak
35 Alabama Ave.
L.I. Park, New York 11558

Chart-Pak, Inc. ("Deca-dry" Dry Transfer)
128DA River Road
Leeds, Massachusetts 01053

Prestype
136 W. 21st St.
New York, N.Y. 10011

Tablet and Ticket Co. (gummed paper, from 1/8" to 4")
1021 W. Adams St.
Chicago, Illinois

APOTHECARY JARS

Kenbury Glass Works
205 W. 19th St.
New York, N.Y. 10011

ARTIFICIAL FOLIAGE

Allied Display Materials, Inc.
241 W. 23rd St.
New York, N.Y. 10011

Arts and Flowers Displays, Inc.
234 W. 56th St.
New York, N.Y. 10019

Evergreen Specialty Co.
Box 868
Denver, Colorado 80201

General Display Co.
25 Opera Place
Cincinnati 2, Ohio

Sidney Newhoff Associates
1200 So. Figueroa St.
Los Angeles, California 90015

ART SUPPLY STORES

American Handicraft Co.
1001 Foch St.
Ft. Worth, Texas 76107

Arthur Brown and Bro., Inc.
2 W. 46th St.
New York, N.Y. 10036

Artists Supply Co.
3194 E. 65 St.
Cleveland, Ohio 44127

A.I. Friedman, Inc.
25 W. 45 St.
New York, N.Y. 10036

H.R. Meininger, Co.
1415 Tremont Pl.
Denver, Colorado 80202

ARTIFICIAL SNOW

Bonafide Display and Decorating Co.
34 W. 38th St.
New York, N.Y. 10018

Garrison-Wagner, Co.
2018 Washington Ave.
St. Louis 3, Mo.

Sloan, Inc.
365 Thatford Ave.
Brooklyn, N.Y. 10012

U.S. Mica Co., Inc.
1525 Circle Ave.
Forest Park, Illinois

BACKGROUNDS

Artistic Latex Form Co., Inc.
1220 Brook Ave.
Bronx, N.Y. 10056

Austen Display, Inc.
133 W. 19th St.
New York, N.Y. 10011

Columbia Display Materials Co.
179 Pacific St.
Brooklyn, N.Y.

Provost Displays, Inc.
618 W. 28th St.
New York, N.Y. 10001

CANVAS

John Boyle and Co., Inc.   (large sizes -- up to 10'
112 Duane St.   wide)
New York, N.Y. 10007

CARD and MAT BOARD

Bainbridge
20 Cumberland St.
Brooklyn, N.Y. 11205

Card and Mat Board (Cont.)

Bulkton, Inc.
2011 W. 12th St.
Erie, Pa.

Butler Paper Mills
323 W. Polk St.
Chicago, Illinois 60607

Crescent Cardboard Co.
1240 No. Homan Ave.
Chicago, Illinois 60651

Miller Cardboard
75 Wooster St.
New York, N.Y. 10012

National Card, Mat and Board Co.
4318 W. Carroll Ave.
Chicago, Illinois 60624

Standard American Matboard
5620 Depster St.
Morton Grove, Illinois 60053

Wilson Paper Co., Inc.
Box 725
Richmond, Virginia 23206

CORRUGATED MATERIALS

Bulkton, Inc.
2011 W. 12th St.
Erie, Pa.

Denton Co.
114 Lincoln St.
Boston, Mass.

DECORATIVE PAPERS

Amscan, Inc.
30 Grove Ave.
New Rochelle, N.Y.

Butler Paper Mills
323 W. Polk St.
Chicago, Illinois 60607

Decorative Papers (Cont.)

Trim Corporation of America
657 Broadway
New York, N.Y. 10012

DISPLAY FIXTURES

Atlantic Plastics Co.
376 Boylston St.
Boston 16, Mass.

Downing Displays
300 Genessee St.
Cincinnati, Ohio 45202

General Display Corp.
25 Opera Pl.
Cincinnati, Ohio 45202

Morrissey Displays and Models
52 Sintsink Drive East
Port Washington, N.Y.

Plastic Fabricators
127 W. 24th St.
New York, N.Y. 10011

Silvestri Art Mfg. Co.
1147 W. Ohio St.
Chicago 22, Illinois

Standard Fixture Co., Inc.
2461 No. Stemmons
Dallas, Texas 75202

Visual Sales Co.
80 Herbert Ave.
Closter, N.J.

World Display Fixtures Corp.
54 Franklin St.
Brooklyn 22, N.Y.

DRY-MOUNTING EQUIPMENT and MATERIALS

Fasson Products (Double-stick, pressure-sensitive,
250 Chester St.   cold type adhesive sheets)
Painesville, Ohio 44077

Seal, Inc. (Presses, tacking irons, tissue)
Shelton, Connecticut

EPOXIES

Bergen Arts and Crafts
Shetland Industrial Park, Box 689
Salem, Mass. 01970

Borden Chemical Co.
350 Madison Ave.
New York, N.Y. 10017

Crystal Craft Center
2849 W. Montrose
Chicago, Illinois 60618

duPont de Nemours & Co.
1007 Market St.
Wilmington, Delaware 19898

Fry Plastics
914 So. Hoover St.
Los Angeles, California 90006

Illinois Bronze Powder and Paint
300 E. Main St.
Lake Zurich, Illinois 60047

Jedco Chemical Corp.
601 N. MacQuesten Pky.
Mt. Vernon, N.Y. 10552

Plasticrafts
2800 No. Speer Blvd.
Denver, Colorado 80211

FABRICS

Associated Fabrics Corp.
10 E. 39th St.
New York, N.Y. 10016

Bulkton, Inc.
2011 W. 12th St.
Erie, Pa.

L.E. Carpenter and Co   (Vicrtex)
350 Fifth Ave., Suite 4202-3
New York, N.Y. 10001

Dazian's Inc.
40 E. 29th St.
New York, N.Y. 10016

Fabrics (Cont.)

Electra Display and Sales Co.
275 Fifth Ave.
New York, N.Y. 10016

Lorraine Fibre Mills, Inc. (colored burlap)
430 Bond St.
Brooklyn 31, N.Y.

Maharam Fabric Corp.
130 W. 46th St.
New York, N.Y. 10036

Van Arden Fabrics, Inc. (colored burlap)
9 No. Moore St.
New York, N.Y. 10013

FLOAT DECORATIONS

Decorative Novelty Co., Inc.
4410 Third Ave.
Brooklyn 20, N.Y.

Frankel Associates, Inc.
202 Fifth Ave.
New York, N.Y. 10010

FLOCKING SUPPLIES

Boin Arts and Crafts Co.
91 Morris St.
Morristown, N.J. 07960

Arthur Brown & Bro., Inc.
2 W. 46th St.
New York, N.Y. 10036

H.R. Meininger Co.
1415 Tremont Pl.
Denver, Colorado 80202

Evergreen Specialty Co.
Box 868
Denver, Colorado 80201

FOUNTAINS (recirculating)

Electra Display and Sales Co.
275 Fifth Ave.
New York, N.Y. 10016

GLASS (non-reflecting, picture frame)

Dearborn Glass
6600 So. Harlem Ave.
Bedford Park P.O.
Argo, Illinois 60501

International Sales Co.
101 So. Hanover St.
Baltimore, Maryland 21201

LATEX

Latex Laboratories, Inc. (L & L Molding Compound)
2336 No. Hayne Ave.
Chicago 47, Illinois

LIGHTING FIXTURES

Alda Inc.
110 Goodale St.
Peabody, Mass. 01960

Amplex Corp.
214 Glen Cove Rd.
Carle Place, N.Y. 11514

Brewster Corp.
Old Lyme, Connecticut 06371

Festive Illumination
938 Port Washington Blvd.
Port Washington, N.Y.

E.H. Friedrichs, Co.
140 Sullivan St.
New York, N.Y. 10012

Halo Lighting, Inc.
9301 W. Bryn Mawr Ave.
Rosemont, Illinois 60018

International Sales
101 So. Hanover St.
Baltimore, Maryland 21201

Lighting Services, Inc.
77 Park Ave.
New York, N.Y. 10016

Lighting Fixtures (Cont.)

  Lightolier
  Jersey City, N.J.

  Northern Light
  1661 No. Water St.
  Milwaukee, Wisconsin 53202

  Swivelier Co.
  33 Route 304
  Nanuet, New York 10954

  Zone Display Fixtures Mfg. Co.
  1100 W. 11th St.
  Los Angeles, California 90015

METAL (Expanded and Gratings)

  Croname, Inc.   (Patterned, textured tubing)
  Chicago, Illinois

  Designers Metal Division of Southern Electric
  8701 So. Greenwood Ave.,
  Chicago 19, Illinois

  Exmet Fine Expanded Metals (Lightweight metals
      for decorative effect)

    Exmet Corp.
    127 Marbledale Road
    Tuckahoe, N.Y.

  Harrington and King, Perforating Co., Inc.
  5664 Fillmore St., Chicago 44, Illinois
                  also
  108 Liberty St.
  New York, N.Y. 10006

PANEL MATERIALS (For panels, cases, and case furniture

  Cellotex (Insulating building board made from sugar
      cane fibers, excellent for case furniture; sheet
      1/2"x4'x8')

    Cellotex Corp.
    120 LaSalle St.
    Chicago 3, Illinois

Panel Materials (Cont.)

Curvo Wall Panels (3/16" thick wood pulp fibreboard
    with pre-formed curves)

    Gregory, Inc.
    203 No. Wabash
    Chicago 1, Illinois

Fomecor (extremely lightweight panel of expanded poly-
    styrene plastic -- similar to styrofoam -- both sides
    clad with Kraft paper; thicknesses of 1/8" and 1/4")

    Fome-Cor Corporation
    812 Monsanto Ave.
    Springfield, Massachusetts

Hardboards (similar to Masonite; some decorative cut-out
    panels)

    Georgia-Pacific, Dept. DW-962-14
    Equitable Bldg.
    Portland 4, Oregon

Homasote (Insulating board in sheets up to 8'x14'. Ask
    for catalogue, samples, and pamphlet on specifica-
    tions and instructions)

    Homasote Company
    Trenton 3, N.J.

Masonite

    Masonite Corporation
    111 W. Washington St.
    Chicago 2, Illinois

Panelaire (Hardboard grillwork)

    Board Products Mfg. Co., Inc., Dept. K
    272 Thomas St.
    Newark, N.J.

Plyboard

    American Plywood Association
    1119 A St.
    Tacoma, Washington 98401

Plywood Filigree Panels

    Maharam Fabric Corp.
    130 W. 46th St.
    New York, N.Y. 10036

Panel Materials (Cont.)

Simpson Insulating Board (Similar to Cellotex, but made of fir fibers)

Simpson Timber Co.,
2000 Washington Bldg.
Seattle, Washington

Upson Board (4'x8' sheets of heavy cardboard-like material, in thicknesses from 1/8" -- called "Easy-Curve" -- to 3/8". Ask for free booklet on display and sample kit of Upson display materials)

Upson Company
Upson Point
Lockport, New York

PLASTICS

Deko Products East (DekoPanel: fiberglas panels 4'x8' in patterns of used brick, Norman brick, Palos Verdes stone, and Texas limestone)

Deko Products
69 Gillett St.
Hartford 5, Connecticut

Fiberglas panels and others -- translucent material with embedded leaves, butterflies, etc.

Filon Plastics Corp.
333 No. Van Ness Ave.
Hawthorne, California

Lucite

Dow Chemical
Midland, Michigan

Plexiglass

Rohm and Haas Co.
Washington Square
Philadelphia 5, Pa.

SCHOOL SUPPLIES

American School Supply Co.
2301 Blake St.
Denver, Colorado 80202

STORAGE EQUIPMENT

Akro-Mils
Box 989
Akron, Ohio 44309

Art Metal
5665 Prince St.
Jamestown, N.Y. 14701

Lyon Metal
Box 671
Aurora, Illinois 60507

STRUCTURAL SYSTEMS

AIM Brand Slotted Steel Angle (Precision drilled steel
    angle bolts together to form very strong supports.
    Up to 10, 12, and 15-foot lengths.

    Acme Steel Co., Chicago 27, Illinois

Alumaline   (Extruded Aluminum framing.)

    Spacesaver Hardware Co., Inc.
    699 Sixth Ave.
    New York, N.Y. 10010

Apton Tube Construction System (Square tube framing
    material assembled just with the use of a mallet.)

    Dexion
    3864 So. Santa Fe Ave.
    Los Angeles, California 90058

Jiffy Clips (Tees and crosses stamped of heavy cold-rolled
    steel; clamp to 1" tubing and plyboard panels to make
    display support.)

    Lodi Tent and Awning Co.
    111 W. Pine St.
    Lodi, California

Key-Pole (Lightweight, spring-loaded aluminum pole for display use.)

    Creative Promotions of California, Inc.
    3820 Grove St.
    Oakland 9, California

Structural Systems (Cont.)

Omni (Solid, anodized aluminum extruded poles to 13' length.)

Structural Products
Charlotte, Michigan

Polecats (Similar to Key-Pole)

Polecats, Inc.
Old Saybrook, Connecticut

System Abstracta (Modular system)

Austen Display, Inc.
133 W. 19th St.
New York, N.Y. 10011

Timber Toppers (Spring-loaded metal "caps" for 2x3 lumber, permits turning any length of 2x3 into a spring-loaded pole for display support. Cost is fraction of other systems.)

Brewster Corporation
Old Lyme, Connecticut 06371

Unistrut Products (Modular structures)

Unistrut Products Co.
1013 W. Washington Blvd.
Chicago 7, Illinois

Walker Display-Divider System (Panels and stands)

Walker
365 So. 1st Ave. East
Duluth, Minnesota 55802

STYROFOAM

Central Plastics Dist.
527 So. Wells St.
Chicago, Illinois 6067

Styro Materials
2519 Walnut St.
Denver, Colorado 80202

TEE-NUTS

A & I Bolt and Nut Co.
1101 Bannock St.
Denver, Colorado 80202

TURNTABLES

Electro-Motion Corp.
Buchanan, N.Y. 10511

Kelley Specialty Mfg. Co.   (Rotaseller)
Box 106-D
Columbus, Kansas 66725

Vue-More Corp.
201 Broad St.
Carlstadt, N.J.

WHERE TO WRITE FOR PRODUCT INFORMATION (if manufacturer is not known)

Editor: DISPLAY WORLD
         407 Gilbert Ave.
         Cincinnati, Ohio 45202

ADDENDUM to Suppliers and Manufacturers List

EXHIBIT CASES

Central Displays, Inc.
1318 Tenth St.
Denver, Colorado 80204

Kewaunee Scientific Equipment Corp.
Adrian, Michigan

The Michaels Art Bronze Co.
P. O. Box 668
Covington, Kentucky

PLASTIC U-V TUBING

Ray Shield Tubing 403
Westlake Plastic Co.
West Lenni Road
Lenni Mills, Pennsylvania 19052

USEFUL PUBLICATIONS

Arnheim, Rudolf. *Art and Visual Perception*. University of California Press, Berkley and Los Angeles, California, 1960.

Baker, Frank and Edward S. Morse. *Visual Communications: International*. Communication Arts Books; Hastings House, Publishers, N.Y., 1961.

Bernard, Frank J. *Dynamic Display*. Display Publishing Co., Cincinnati, Ohio, 1952.

Better Homes & Gardens Handyman's Book. Meredith Publishing Co., 1957.

"Big Leisure-Time Explosion," in *Popular Gardening and Living Outdoors*, Spring 1968. Holt, Rinehart and Winston, Inc., N.Y.

Birren, Faber. *Selling With Color*. McGraw-Hill, N.Y., 1945.

————— —————. *Color, Form and Space*. Reinhold Publishing Corp. N.Y., 1961.

Black, Mischa, ed. *Exhibition Design*. Architectural Press, London, 1950.

Borgwardt, Stephanie. *Library Display*. Witwatersrand University Press, Johannesburg, South Africa, 1960.

Buckley, Jim. *The Drama of Display*. Pellegrini & Cudahy, New York, 1953.

Burns, Ned. *Field Manual for Museums*. National Park Service, Washington, D.C., 1941.(out of print).

Butkowski, Patricia. *A Look You'll Like in Labels*. Detroit Historical Society, Detroit, Michigan, 1960.

Campbell, Robert and N.H. Mager. *How to Work With Tools and Wood*. Pocket Books, Inc., N.Y., 1965.

Carmel, James. *Exhibition Techniques*. Reinhold Publishing Co., N.Y., 1962.

Coleman, L. V. *The Museum in America*. (3 vols.) American Association of Museums, Washington, D.C., 1939.

————— —————. *Museum Buildings*. American Association of Museums, Washington, D.C., 1950.

Cummings, Carlos. *East is East and West is West*. Buffalo
   Museum of Science, Buffalo, N.Y., 1940.

Dair, Carl. *Design With Type*. Pellegrini & Cudahy, N.Y., 1952.

Dale, Edgar. *Audio-Visual Methods in Teaching*. Dryden Press, N.Y., 1954.

Daniels, George. *How to Be Your Own Home Electrician*. Popular
   Science Publishing Co., Harper & Row, N.Y., 1967.

DeCristoforo, R.J. *How to Build Your Own Furniture*. Popular
   Science Publishing Co., Harper & Row, N.Y., 1967.

Dennison Flower Book. Dennison Mfg. Co., Framingham, Mass., 1959.

Dreyfuss, Henry. *Designing for People*. Simon and Schuster, N.Y., 1955.

————— ———. *The Measure of Man*. Whitney Library of Design,
   Whitney Publications, Inc., N.Y., 1960.

Exhibition Techniques. New York Museum of Science and Industry.
   Rockefeller Center, N.Y., 1940.

Flesch, Rudolf. *The Art of Readable Writing*. Harper & Bros., N.Y., 1949.

Gaba, Lester. *The Art of Window Display*. Studio Publications,
   Thos. Y. Crowell Co., N.Y., 1952.

Gardner and Heller. *Exhibition and Display*. F. W. Dodge Corp., N.Y., 1960.

Garrett, Lillian. *Visual Design*. Reinhold Publishing Corp., N.Y., 1967.

Guthe, Carl. *So You Want a Good Museum*. American Association of
   Museums, Washington, D.C., 1957.

Hayett, William. *Display and Exhibit Handbook*. Reinhold Publishing Corp., N.Y., 1967.

Horn, George F. *Bulletin Boards*. Reinhold Publishing Corp., N.Y., 1962.

Kapp, Reginald O. *The Presentation of Technical Information*. Mac-
   millan Co., N.Y., 1948.

Kane, Lucile M. *A Guide to Care and Administration of Manuscripts*.
   American Association for State and Local History, Nashville,
   Tennessee , 1966.

Leroi-Gourhan, A. *Prehistoric Man*. Philosophical Library, N.Y., 1957.

Lohse, Richard P. *New Design in Exhibitions*. Praeger, Inc., N.Y., 1954.

196

Lonberg-Holm and Sutnar. *Designing Information*. Whitney Publications, Inc., N.Y., 1947.

Longyear, William. *Type and Lettering*. Watson-Guptill Publications, Inc., N.Y., 1965.

Low. *The Museum As a Social Instrument*. American Association of Museums, Washington, D.C., 1942.

Luckiesh, M. *Visual Illusions*. Dover Publications, Inc., N.Y., 1965.

Manual of Exhibit Properties. Detroit Historical Museum. Detroit, Michigan, 1961.

Marshall, William E. and Robert L. Damm. *The Museum Exhibit*. Ohio Historical Society, Ohio State Museum, Columbus, Ohio, 1959.

Neal, Arminta. *Cigar Box Dioramas*. Denver Museum of Natural History, Denver, Colorado, 1958.

————— —————. "New Uses for Styrofoam Plastic in Museum Display" in *Curator*, Vol. 5, No. 2; 1962, American Museum of Natural History, New York, N.Y.

Nelms, Henning. *Thinking With a Pencil*. Barnes & Noble, Inc., N.Y., 1974.

Nelson, George. *Display*. Whitney Publications, N.Y., 1953.

The Organization of Museums: Practical Advice. UNESCO: Columbia University Press, New York, N.Y., 1960.

Osborn. *Manual of Travelling Exhibitions*. UNESCO: Columbia University Press, New York, N.Y., 1953.

Panero, Julius. *Anatomy for Interior Designers*. Whitney Publications, Inc., New York, N.Y., 1962.

Parker, Donald Dean. *Local History: How to Gather It, Write It, and Publish It*. Social Science Research Council, New York, N.Y., 1944.

Parr, A.E. *Mostly About Museums*. American Museum of Natural History, New York, N.Y., 1959.

"Planning Museums and Art Galleries," in *Museums Journal*, Vol. 63, Nos. 1 & 2, June-Sept., 1963. The Museums Association, London, England.

Pond, Gordon G. *Science Materials: Preparation and Exhibition for the Classroom*. William C. Brown Co., Publishers, Dubuque, Iowa, 1959.

Publications in Museology:

No. 1   *A Bibliography of Museums and Museum Work, 1900 - 1960*. Stephan F. de Borhegyi and Elba A. Dodson.

No. 2   *A Bibliography of Museums and Museum Work, 1900 - 1961, Supplement*. Stephan F. de Borhegyi, Elba A. Dodson, and Irene A. Hanson.

No. 3   *The Museum Visitor*. Stephan F. de Borhegyi, Irene A. Hanson, eds.

    Milwaukee Public Museum, Milwaukee, Wisconsin.

Randall, Reino and Edward C. Haines. *Bulletin Boards and Display*. Davis Publications, Inc., Worcester, Mass., 1961.

Rowe, Frank A. *Display Fundamentals*. The Display Publishing Co., Cincinnati, Ohio, 1965.

Schwartz, Alvin. *Museum*. E. P. Dutton & Co., Inc., N.Y., 1967.

Science on Display: A Study of the United States Science Exhibit, Seattle World's Fair, 1962. Institute for Sociological Research, University of Washington, Seattle, Washington, 1963.

Shelley, William J. *Paper Sculpture in the Classroom*. Fearon Publishers, San Francisco, California, 1957.

Silvestro, Clement. *Organizing a Local Historical Society*. American Association for State and Local History, Nashville, Tennessee, 1959.

Smith, Paul, ed. *Creativity*. Communication Arts Books, Hastings House, Publishers, N.Y., 1959.

Sutnar, Ladislav. *Visual Design in Action*. Hastings House, N.Y., 1961.

Talmadge, R.H. *Point of Sale Display*. The Studio Publications, N.Y., 1958.

Taylor, Francis Henry. *Babel's Tower*. Columbia University Press, N.Y., 1945.

Technical Leaflets (a continuing series). American Association for State and Local History, Nashville, Tennessee.

Weseloh, Anne D. *E-Z Bulletin Boards*. Fearon Publishers, San Francisco, California, 1959.

Wittlin, Alma. *The Museum: Its History and Its Tasks in Education*. Routledge and Kegan Paul, Ltd., London, 1949.

ADDENDUM to Publications List

Harrison, Raymond O. *The Technical Requirements of Small Museums*. Technical Paper No. 1. Canadian Museums Association, Ottawa, Ontario, 1966.

Long, Charles J. *Museum Workers Notebook*. Witte Museum, San Antonio, Texas, 1964.

Rath, Frederick L. Jr., and Merrilyn Rogers. *Selective Reference Guide to Historic Preservation*. New York State Historical Association, Cooperstown, N. Y., 1966.

ASSOCIATIONS

American Association of Museums
2306 Massachusetts Ave., N. W.
Washington, D. C.

American Association for State and Local History
132 Ninth Ave., North
Nashville, Tennessee

...affiliated with the American Association of Museums are the following regional organizations, information about which may be obtained from the Washington office:

Midwest Museums Conference
Mountain-Plains Museums Conference
New England Regional Conference
New York State Association of Museums
Northeast Regional Museums Conference
Oklahoma Museums Association
Pacific Northwest Museum Conference
Southeastern Museums Conference
Tennessee Association of Museums
Texas Museums Conference
Western Association of Art Museums
Western Museums League

A Note on the preparation of this book:

A camera-ready paste-up for offset printing was
prepared by the author. An IBM "Selectric," 12-pitch
typewriter, was used with the following typing elements:

> LETTER GOTHIC- (for main headings)
> ADJUTANT - (for body text)
> *LIGHT ITALIC - (for captions and emphasis)*

Most photographs were made with Polaroid equipment; many illustrations originated as colored slides
which were enlarged directly onto Polaroid print paper.
All line drawings were prepared by the author.

DATE DUE
